ogues with contemporary

FOR ANNE

'Para dialogar
Preguntad, primero
Despus, escuchad'

(That dialogue may happen,
Ask first,
Then listen)

Antonio Machado

RICHARD KEARNEY

Dialogues with contemporary Continental thinkers

The phenomenological heritage

PAUL RICOEUR

EMMANUEL LEVINAS

HERBERT MARCUSE

STANISLAS BRETON

JACQUES DERRIDA

Manchester University Press

First published 1984
by Manchester University Press
Oxford Road, Manchester M13 9PL
and Room 400, 175 Fifth Avenue,
New York, NY 10010, USA

Distributed exclusively in the USA and Canada
by St. Martin's Press Inc.,
175 Fifth Avenue, New York, NY 10010, USA

Reprinted 1986, 1989

British Library cataloguing in publication data
Kearney, Richard
Dialogues with contemporary continental thinkers
I. Philosophy, Modern—20th century
1. Title.
190 B804
ISBN 0-7190-1729 7 pbk

Library of Congress cataloging in publication data
Kearney, Richard
Dialogues with contemporary continental thinkers.
Includes biographies.
1. Philosophy, Modern—20th century—Addresses, essays, lectures.
I. Ricoeur, Paul. II. Title.
B804.K36 1984 190 84-17162

ISBN 0-7190-1729-7

Printed in Great Britain
by Biddles Ltd., Guildford and King's Lynn

Contents

Acknowledgements

I wish to thank my friends and colleagues, Ronan Sheehan, Patrick Masterson, Joseph O'Leary, Fran O'Rourke and Desmond Connell for their helpful comments and encouragements, my wife Anne for her continual support and companionship, and of course my five partners in dialogue who so generously consented to answer my questions and communicate their philosophical quest.

Author's note

The titles of philosophical works are given in the original language only where an English translation is not yet available. All of the dialogues published here have been translated into English by the author – with the exception of Herbert Marcuse's which was originally conducted in English.

Introduction

This collection of dialogues will, I hope, not only challenge certain misconceptions about modern Continental thought, but also help to clarify some of its more complex or abstruse dimensions. If the common-sense empiricism of Anglo-American philosophy has often found too much to offend in contemporary Continental thinking, there exists the opposite extreme of those who would defend it at all costs and in all cases. Uncritical adulation of anything that hails from Paris, Frankfurt or Freiburg is not likely to help the cause; and there is little doubt that certain phenomenological, structuralist or post-structuralist cliques have recently emerged, which sometimes tend towards a sacralization of their 'new prophets'. But neither faction of the philosophical divide – Anglo-American or Continental – can claim to be on the side of the angels. Self-righteous intolerance of the 'other' is indefensible whatever its geographical or intellectual source.

Through these dialogues with Continental thinkers, I hope to assist in the translation of their respective philosophies into the Anglo-American world of thought. Such a translation will perhaps contribute to the formation of a more comprehensive dialogue between these two intellectual cultures. Much pioneering work has already been begun by philosophers such as Vincent Descombes, Charles Taylor, Alan Montefiori, Paul Ricoeur and others, to bring together the frequently opposed traditions. The present publication is intended as another step in this direction of intellectual *détente* by extending an additional arch to the bridge of intellectual *entente*.

I

The dialogues afford each of the five thinkers an opportunity to introduce, situate and clarify their own work, to speak for themselves as it were. I have included short prefatory notes and bibliographies by way of providing the reader with some additional background information. Suffice it here to say something briefly about my selection of thinkers and then sketch out some of the common contexts and co-ordinates of their respective philosophies.

Our list is by no means comprehensive, but it does, I believe, include philosophers who articulate and illustrate significant and, for the most part, representative movements of contemporary thought: (1) Marcuse: a *critical dialectics* in debate with the Marxist–Hegelian Frankfurt school; (2) Lévinas: an *ethics* in debate with religious metaphysics; (3) Ricoeur: a *hermeneutics* in debate with the human sciences; (4) Derrida: a philosophy of *deconstruction* in debate with structuralism; (5) Breton: a *religious poetics* representing one of the most advanced schools of modern Catholic philosophy in France combining the insights of Thomism, neoplatonism, existentialism and aesthetics.[1]

The five thinkers in dialogue here also represent a variety of nations, cultures and religions of the European continent. Marcuse is a German of Jewish background who began his philosophical work in Freiburg and Frankfurt before moving to the United States; Lévinas is a Lithuanian Jew who has lived most of his life in Paris, though he has also worked in Germany and Israel; Ricoeur is a French Protestant who has lived and worked in Germany, Belgium and the United States as well as France; Breton is a French Catholic who taught for many years at *l'Institut Catholique* in Paris; Derrida is a French Algerian of Jewish origin educated in France where he still teaches at *l'Ecole Normale Supérieure de Paris*.

In the preface to his novel, *Roderick Hudson*, Henry James commented on the author's problematic procedure of establishing relations between the themes, idioms and characters of his work: 'Really, universally, relations stop nowhere, and the exquisite problem of the [author] is eternally to draw, by a geometry of his own, the circle within which they shall appear to do so.' In these remaining paragraphs I wish to sketch some circles of philosophical reference and cross-reference wherein the different works of the five thinkers in dialogue overlap or intersect.

Even though many of the writings of Ricoeur, Derrida and, in particular, Marcuse, have been available in English for some years now, not a great deal has been written in the English-speaking world about the manner in which their respective intellectual projects derive from and develop seminal movements of Continental thought. I am thinking particularly of the formative influence variously exerted upon these thinkers by the three following schools of thought: first, the critical 'hermeneutics of suspicion' – to borrow Ricoeur's phrase – advanced by Hegelian Marxism, Nietzsche and Freud; secondly, the structural linguistics of Saussure, Jacobson, Lévi-Strauss and others; and, most importantly, the phenomenological and existentialist theories developed by Husserl, Heidegger, Marcel, Jaspers, Sartre and Merleau-Ponty.

The phenomenological movement: the first generation

Phenomenology represents the most pervasive common influence for our five thinkers. This is not surprising when one considers that phenomenological existentialism generated the main body of European philosophy between 1930 and 1960, especially in France and Germany, occasioning what many would regard as the 'golden age' of contemporary Continental thought.

The phenomenological movement was inaugurated by the German philosopher, Edmund Husserl, whose deeply influential work, *Logical Investigations*, was published in 1900. In this and subsequent works, Husserl outlined the primary aims and methods of phenomenology. His essential project was to enable philosophy to 'return to the things themselves', by which he meant the *phenomena* of meaning as constituted by human consciousness. Consciousness (*Bewusstsein*) was no longer to be understood in terms of traditional metaphysics or positivism as a given substance or objective fact. A new method, Husserl argued, must be advanced which could disclose, describe and intuit its essential functioning as an *activity of intentionality*. By this he meant that consciousness is always consciousness *of* something other than itself: it now reveals itself as a dynamic act forever projecting itself beyond the idealist enclosures of the mind towards horizons of transcendent meaning. Husserl's phenomenological theory of intentionality led, furthermore, to the discovery that consciousness as a *reflective* logical operation already presupposes a *prereflective* lived experience of the world, what Husserl called the 'lifeworld' (*Lebenswelt*). Only by returning to and investigating this creative nexus *between* consciousness and world, where reality originally and primordially *appears* to us (qua *phenomenon*) in our intentional, lived experience, can we ultimately arrive at an intuition of essential truth: the true *essences* of things themselves.

Husserl's phenomenological investigations served as a radical authority for the subsequent works of Heidegger, Sartre and Merleau-Ponty – to mention only the first generation of Husserl's disciplines. Heidegger's *Being and Time*, published in 1927, was dedicated to Husserl and acknowledged a profound debt to his mentor's pioneering researches. The original contribution to phenomenology made by Heidegger was to rework Husserl's method in the direction of a more existential and ontological analysis of meaning. Whereas Husserl had tended to confine his analyses to an enquiry of the scientific and logical foundations of truth, Heidegger broadened their scope to include a concrete description of man's finite being-in-the-world (*In-der-Welt-Sein*). Only by thus concentrating on the existential moods, cares and projects of our being-there (*Da-Sein*) in historical time, might we eventually be in a position to ask once again the most fundamental of all philosophical questions: *What does it mean to be?* Human temporality as concretely lived and described emerged for Heidegger as the indispensable horizon of the question of Being itself.

These 'essentialist' and 'existentialist' versions of phenomenology, advanced by Husserl and Heidegger respectively, were refashioned in even more engaging idioms by such 'first-generation' French phenomenologists as Sartre and Merleau-Ponty. Sartre's *Being and Nothingness* (1943) offered a wide variety of vivid phenomenological descriptions of human existence as an intentional project of action, freedom, choice and responsibility. And this approach found its most popular and controversial expression in his 'philosophy of commitment' sketched out in *Existentialism and Humanism* (1947). It was in these early works that Sartre – aided and abetted by Camus' *Myth of Sisyphus* (1942) – was to set the philosophical tone for his generation by declaring that man's 'existence precedes his essence' since man is 'responsible for everything he does', 'makes himself what he is' and is thus 'condemned to be free'.

Merleau-Ponty's principal work *The Phenomenology of Perception* (1945) developed the methods of Husserl and Heidegger in a similarly *engagé* manner; its primary purpose being the description of our situated existence as 'body-subjects' who creatively *experience* our world before we ever actually *analyse* it in abstract, scientific terms. Merleau-Ponty hailed phenomenology as being 'destined to bring back all the living relationships of experience, as the fisherman's net draws up from the depths of the ocean quivering fish and seaweed'.[2] He identified the compelling force of such an open-ended and exploratory philosophy for the eager minds of the modern generation as follows:

> We shall find in ourselves and nowhere else, the unity and true meaning of phenomenolgy. It is less a question of counting up quotations than of determining and expressing in concrete form this *phenomenology for ourselves* which has given a number of present-day readers the impression, on reading Husserl and Heidegger, not so much of encountering a new philosophy as of recognizing what they had been waiting for . . . The unfinished nature of phenomenology and the inchoative atmosphere which has surrounded it are not to be taken as a sign of failure, they were inevitable because phenomenology's task was to reveal the mystery of the world and of reason. If phenomenology was a movement before becoming a doctrine or a philosophical system, this was attributable neither to accident, nor to fraudulent intent. It is as painstaking as the works of Balzac, Proust, Valéry or Cézanne – by reason of the same kind of attentiveness and wonder, the same demand for awareness, the same will to seize the meaning of the world or of history as that meaning comes into being. In this way it merges into the general effort of modern thought.[3]

Parallel to this mainstream movement of phenomenological existentialism emerged the 'Christian existentialism' of Karl Jaspers (whose three-volume *Philosophie* appeared in 1931) and of Gabriel Marcel (whose more 'personalist' study *The Philosophy of Existence* was published in 1936). This particular brand of existentialist thinking also held a profound attraction for several of the 'second generation' of Continental thinkers – perhaps most notably Paul Ricoeur.

It is clear, moreover, that both groupings of first-generation existentialists – phenomenological and non-phenomenological alike – shared a common debt, albeit in varying degrees, to such nineteenth-century existentialist writers as Kierkegaard, Nietzsche or Dostoyevsky, writers whose primary concern it was to challenge the impersonal and reified systems of traditional, speculative philosophies in the name of the concrete freedom of each individual's existence.

The phenomenological heritage: the second generation

Even though Lévinas, Ricoeur and Marcuse were already reading, and indeed writing about, the philosophy of Husserl and Heidegger in the thirties, forties and fifties, it was not really until the sixties that they succeeded in transforming their initial, largely critical, researches into works that proved original and influential in their own right. Thus, for example, though Lévinas was in fact the first to introduce Sartre to phenomenology, with the publication of his *La Théorie de l'intuition dans la phénoménologie de Husserl*, which appeared in France as early as 1930, and though he published a study entitled *En découvrant l'existence avec Husserl et Heidegger* in 1949, it was not until the appearance of some twelve major works between 1960 and 1980 – beginning with his monumental *Totality and Infinity* (1961) – that Lévinas firmly established himself as a major contemporary thinker helping to readjust the intellectual tone for the second generation of Continental phenomenologists.

We find a similar pattern in the *curriculum vitae* of Ricoeur's own remarkable contribution to phenomenology and existentialism. Ricoeur began by publishing critical commentaries on Jaspers and Marcel (1948) and Husserl (1950). But it was undoubtedly with the publication of the second volumes of his phenomenological *Philosophy of Will* in 1960, followed by his two major works on phenomenological hermeneutics, *Freud and Philosophy: An Essay on Interpretation* (1965) and *The Conflict of Interpretations* (1969), that he was ultimately acknowledged as one of the most significant philosophers of the post-fifties period.

For his part, Marcuse's seminal studies on phenomenological hermeneutics and critical theory in the late twenties and early thirties (when he, like Lévinas, studied with Husserl and Heidegger in Freiburg, before moving to the Frankfurt School of Social Research), did not come to full fruition until the sixties and seventies when his books, particularly *One-dimensional Man* (1964) and *An Essay on Liberation* (1969), came to fascinate the young and rebellious generation of 1968.

The two other thinkers in dialogue here, Derrida and Breton, also acknowledge a debt to phenomenology and/or existentialism. Since this debt is made explicit in the dialogues themselves, there is no need to expand upon it here. Suffice it just to mention in passing Breton's phenomenological studies of the intentional relationship between consciousness and Being; and Derrida's 'deconstructive' reinterpretations of Husserl and Heidegger (beginning with his two first major publications: *Edmund Husserl's 'Origin of Geometry': An Introduction* (1962) and *Speech and Phenomena and Other Essays in Husserl's Theory of Signs* (1967)).

But whatever our five thinkers in dialogue may have derived from the first generation of phenomenologists, they have each succeeded in refashioning this heritage according to their own original image – often indeed to the extent of surpassing it altogether. One could perhaps venture a summary of their respective debts to the phenomenological movement in terms of the following basic, if somewhat simplified, descriptions: Ricoeur – hermeneutic phenomenology; Lévinas – ethical phenomenology; Breton – poetic or religious phenomenology; Marcuse – dialectical phenomenology; Derrida – deconstructive phenomenology. In short, despite their later differences, all five thinkers would appear to share an original phenomenological starting-point: that is, the conviction that a radical interrogation of *meaning* requires us to penetrate beneath the established concepts of empirical, logical or scientific 'objectivication' (what Husserl called the 'natural attitude') to that concretely 'lived experience' of man's temporal and historical *being-in-the-world*. All five began with the view that philosophical *signification* always presupposes the *signifying* activity of our intentional consciousness; and that any attempt to abstract or isolate signification from this prior activity results in the 'reification' or 'mystification' of our understanding.

I have confined the preceding 'comparative' remarks to the movement of phenomenological existentialism, believing it to be the single most pervasive influence on the thinkers featured in this collection. I would not wish to underestimate, however, the substantial, albeit sporadic, influence of the two other formative movements mentioned above: the *hermeneutics of suspicion* and *structural analysis*. The innovative theories of Saussure or Lévi-Strauss, for example, recur as critical references throughout the writings of

Ricoeur and Derrida. Freud – as one instance of the 'hermeneutics of suspicion' – occupies a central place in the analyses of Marcuse, Ricoeur and Derrida; and the Marxist–Hegelian dialectic – as another instance of such a hermeneutics – plays a pivotal role in the critiques of ideology advanced by Marcuse, Breton, Ricoeur, Derrida and also, though less directly, in the anti-totalitarian ethics of Lévinas. Once again, I refer the reader to the thinkers' own remarks on these matters in their respective dialogues.

II

I have chosen the dialogue format because it fosters communication and may thus facilitate the reader's grasp of the philosophical problems under discussion. Continental thinkers are often extremely difficult to understand. Part of this difficulty is, I believe, inherent in the very nature of the metaphysical or epistemological questioning in which these thinkers are engaged. And this is particularly true in the case of the phenomenological terms variously employed by the thinkers I dialogue with here. Martin Heidegger, one of the founders of the phenomenological movement, acknowledged the essential difficulty raised by his own use of innovatory philosophical language in his Introduction to *Being and Time* (1927):

> With regard to the awkwardness and 'inelegance' of expression in the analyses to come, we may remark that it is one thing to give a report in which we tell about *entities* (i.e. familiar objects), but another to grasp entities in their Being. For the latter task we lack not only most of the words but, above all, the 'grammar'. If we may allude to some earlier researchers on the analysis of Being, incomparable on their own level, we may compare the ontological sections of Plato's *Parmenides*, or the fourth chapter of the seventh book of Aristotle's *Metaphysics* with a narrative section from Thucydides; we can then see the altogether unprecedented character of those formulations which were imposed upon the Greeks by their philosophers. And where our powers are essentially weaker, and where moreover the area of Being to be disclosed is ontologically far more difficult than that which was presented to the Greeks, the harshness of our expression will be enhanced, and so will the minuteness of detail with which our concepts are formed.[4]

This explanation applies with equal validity to the original analyses in phenomenological hermeneutics, poetics and deconstruction produced by the respective thinkers included in this book.

This terminological difficulty may be more simply expressed in Marcuse's terms: a one-dimensional language can only deal with a one-dimensional reality, whereas it is the critical duty of philosophy to explore and interrogate *other*, and perhaps hitherto undisclosed, dimensions of existence and truth.[5]

The attempts to purge philosophical language of its metaphysical or critical dimensions in order to reduce it to the cut-and-dried clarity of formal logic or the common-sense accessibility of ordinary language are sometimes of a restrictive nature. The refusal to extend analysis beyond the parameters of 'ordinary discourse' may in fact bespeak a refusal to open up a new and qualitatively different universe which might well contradict or contest our established ordinary universe. As Marcuse remarked, adverting to the ideological as well as metaphysical dangers of such linguistic reductionism: 'The metaphysical dimension, formerly a genuine field of rational thought, becomes irrational and unscientific . . . The contemporary effort to reduce the scope and the truth of philosophy is tremendous and the philosophers themselves proclaim the modesty and inefficacy of philosophy. It leaves the established reality untouched; it abhors transgression.'[6] By attending exclusively to the given *facts* of ordinary language, one runs the risk of ignoring the metaphysical or socio-historic *factors* which lie behind and precondition these facts. The following passages from Marcuse's *One-dimensional Man* (1964) identify the shortcomings of efforts to eradicate the novelty and unfamiliarity of much genuine philosophical discourse:

> The almost masochistic reduction of speech to the humble and common is made into a program . . . Thinking (or at least its expression) is not only pressed into the straight-jacket of common usage, but also enjoined not to ask and seek solutions beyond those that are already there . . . One might ask what remains of philosophy? What remains of thinking, intelligence, without any explanation? However, what is at stake is not the definition or the dignity of philosophy. It is rather the chance of preserving and protecting the right, the *need* to think and to speak in terms other than those of common usage – terms which are meaningful, rational and valid precisely because they are *other* terms . . . An irreducible difference exists between the universe of everyday thinking and language on the one side, and that of philosophical thinking and language on the other . . . The neo-positivist critique still directs its main effort against metaphysical notions, and it is motivated by a notion of exactness which is either that of formal logic or empirical description. Whether exactness is sought in the analytic purity of logic

> and mathematics, or in conformity with ordinary language – on both poles of contemporary philosophy is the same rejection or devaluation of those elements of thought and speech which transcend the accepted system of validation . . . In its exposure of the mystifying character of transcendent terms, vague notions, metaphysical universals and the like, linguistic analysis mystifies the terms of ordinary language by leaving them in the repressive context of the established universe of discourse . . . In this analytic treatment of ordinary language the latter is really sterilized and anaesthetized. Multi-dimensional language is made into one-dimensional language, in which different and conflicting meanings no longer interpenetrate but are kept apart; the explosive historical dimension of meaning is silenced.[7]

I have quoted Marcuse at such length because I believe that his more ideological explanation of the difficulties involved in genuine thinking, coupled with Heidegger's ontological explanation, represents an essential caveat to any facile effort to 'explain away' the fundamental complexities of much Continental philosophy.[8]

In acknowledging the difficulties of Continental philosophy, however, I would reiterate that one of the primary purposes of this book is to offer clarification – without resorting to one-dimensional reductionism. I have endeavoured in these dialogues to enable the thinkers in question to respond to critiques levelled against them and to spell out, where possible, the key concepts and arguments of their work. My intention here – and I have no doubt that of my interlocutors also – is to explain and simplify wherever it seems legitimate to do so without being simplistic; without, that is, betraying the innovatory richness of the philosophies discussed.

I hope that this exegetical scruple might also serve to ensure that this publication will not be confined to university specialists or professional philosophers but will prove accessible to non-academic readers interested in modern Continental thought and prepared to make the extra effort required to comprehend that which may not always appear immediately comprehensible.

For those who remain sceptical of any discourse which transcends the 'analytic treatment of ordinary language', perhaps the best attitude to adopt in entering into these somewhat unfamiliar dialogues is that recommended by the poet, Samuel Coleridge: 'a willing suspension of disbelief'.

Notes

1. There are many other influential thinkers on the Continent whom one might reasonably expect to see included here – Barthes, Lévi-Strauss, Lacan, Foucault, Lyotard, Lefort, Gadamer, Habermas, Desanti, Kristeva, Serres or Girard. But, as Spinoza taught, *omnis determinatio est negatio*: any determination of inclusion necessarily involves exclusion. My particular selection in this book does not express a conviction that these five are indisputably the most significant or the most representative of contemporary Continental thinkers. I do believe, however, that they are each of them significant and representative in some important respect. Indeed, those thinkers featured here who might not immediately strike an English-speaking reader as fulfilling a representative role – perhaps Lévinas or Breton – do merit inclusion, I feel, if only by way of helping to make their still largely unfamiliar work that bit more available to an Anglo-American readership. Moreover, the relative unfamiliarity of such thinkers in our world in no way detracts from their representative status on the Continent. All five, of course, share a common debt to a phenomenological formation and thereby represent a coherent grouping.
2. Maurice Merleau-Ponty, *The Phenomenology of Perception*, transl. C. Smith. Routledge and Kegan Paul, London, 1962, Preface, p. xv.
3. *Ibid.*, pp. viii, xxi.
4. Martin Heidegger, *Being and Time*, transl. J. Macquarrie and E. Robinson. Blackwell, Oxford, 1973, p. 63.
5. Herbert Marcuse, *One-dimensional Man: Studies in the Ideology of Advanced Industrial Society*. Beacon Press, Boston, 1964, pp. 123 *et seq.*
6. *Ibid.*, p. 173.
7. *Ibid.*, pp. 177, 182, 184, 199.
8. It is, of course, a tribute to Marcuse himself that he can articulate his arguments in so direct a manner. No doubt Marcuse's familiarity with the English-language – and, by implication, Anglo-American thought – has made easier the 'translation' and transmission of his own dialectical philosophy. Forty years or so working in American universities, since his flight from Nazi Germany in the thirties, certainly facilitated this task. Others of his dialectical Hegelian–Marxist ilk – notably Adorno, Benjamin or Horkheimer – are less known or read outside of the Continent. Despite the fact, however, that Marcuse has written almost as many books in English as in German, and has done more than most to grant Marx, Hegel and phenomenology a legitimate currency in the Anglo-American sphere, there are still many who regard his work as terminologically obscure and conceptually diffuse.

Dialogues

Paul Ricoeur

Prefatory note

Paul Ricoeur was born in Valence, France, in 1913. During his captivity in Germany during the war, Ricoeur taught philosophy to his fellow prisoners and familiarized hiself with German phenomenology and existentialism. On his return to France, he pursued his interest in the philosophy of subjectivity and existence, publishing works on *Gabriel Marcel and Karl Jaspers* in 1948; on *Karl Jaspers and the Philosophy of Existence* (with Mikel Dufrenne) in 1947; and on Husserl's *Ideas*, together with a translation, in 1950. In 1948, Ricoeur was appointed Professor of the History of Philosophy at the University of Strasbourg, where he remained until 1956 when he moved to Paris, serving as Professor of Metaphysics at both the Sorbonne (1956–66) and Nanterre (1966–80). He still holds a post as John Nuveen Professor at the University of Chicago where he has taught part-time since 1960.

Ricoeur's most original and influential contribution to contemporary thinking has been his *Philosophy of Will*, three volumes of which have already appeared – *The Voluntary and the Involuntary* (1950), *Fallible Man* (1960) and *The Symbolism of Evil* (1960). In these works of his middle period, Ricoeur argues that the ideal of a self-transparent, autonomous subjectivity promoted by Descartes' idealism of the *cogito* and Husserl's idealism of the transcendental ego, is ultimately impossible. The human will, he claims, is always confronted by the 'involuntary' limits of finitude which defy or exceed its subjective powers. The subject can never lay claim, therefore, to pure, immediate self-reflection; it is always traversed by meanings other than its own; it is a decentred, split, fallible *cogito* which finds itself in a world whose meaning largely precedes its own voluntary initiatives. And so Ricoeur points to the necessity to move from a pure phenomenology of reflective consciousness to a hermeneutic phenomenology which recognizes that the subject's retrieval of itself and of meaning requires a 'detour' through the 'objective' structures of culture, religion, society and language. He defines hermeneutics accordingly as 'the art of deciphering indirect meanings'. Only by clearly acknowledging the existence of such trans-subjective barriers to our subjective projects can we finally hope to interpret these 'mediations' in the light of the ultimate goals of freedom and understanding (what Ricoeur refers to as a 'teleology' or 'eschatology' of the subject).

It is just such a hermeneutic detour through the alienating and mediating structures of meaning which Ricoeur undertakes in *The Symbolism of Evil* and in the later more explicitly hermeneutic works, *Freud and Philosophy: an Essay on Interpretation* (1965), *The Conflict of Interpretations* (1969); and most recently in *The Rule of Metaphor* (1975) and *Temps et récit* (1983). The primary aim of these hermeneutic studies is to show how the classical ideal of absolute knowledge is always deferred or displaced by an endless series of expropriations and reappropriations of meaning (via the notion of the 'unconscious' in psychoanalysis, of anonymous linguistic 'codes' in structuralism or of the impersonal 'facticity' of time and circumstance in the political philosophies of history).

A modern philosophy of consciousness, insists Ricoeur, must enter into dialogue with the human sciences – politics, sociology, linguistics, psychology, history, economics, etc. Only by recognizing the various obstacles and opacities which the project of self-understanding encounters, and by thus resisting the facile solution of some 'absolute synthesis' of knowledge which would contrive to resolve prematurely the conflict of interpretations, can we achieve an authentic grasp of the role of human creativity and imagination in spite of all the odds. In other words, it is only if we take seriously the 'hermeneutics of suspicion', which in Freud, Marx, Nietszche and elsewhere seeks to expose the idealist fallacy of self-transparent consciousness, that we may work towards a 'hermeneutics of affirmation' which continues to believe in the recovery of lost meanings and the creation of new ones – the opening up of 'possible worlds'.

The first of the dialogues that follow was recorded in Paris in 1981 and the second in Paris in 1978.

I: The Creativity of Language

Richard Kearney: How do your recent works on metaphor (*La Métaphore vive*, 1975) and narrativity (*Temps et récit*, 1983) fit into your overall programme of philosophical hermeneutics?

Paul Ricoeur: In *La Métaphore vive* (*The Rule of the Metaphor*) I tried to show how language could extend itself to its very limits forever discovering new resonances within itself. The term *vive* (living) in the title of this work is all important, for it was my purpose to demonstrate that there is not just an epistemological and political imagination, but also, and perhaps more fundamentally, a *linguistic* imagination which generates and regenerates meaning through the living power of metaphoricity. *La Métaphore vive* investigated the resources of rhetoric to show how language undergoes creative mutations and transformations. My work on narrativity, *Temps et récit*, develops this inquiry into the inventive power of language. Here, the analysis of narrative operations in a literary text, for instance, can teach us how we formulate a new structure of 'time' by creating new modes of plot and characterization. My chief concern in this analysis is to discover how the act of *raconter*, of telling a story, can transmute *natural* time into a specifically *human* time, irreducible to mathematical, chronological 'clock time'. How is narrativity, as the construction or deconstruction of paradigms of story-telling, a perpetual search for new ways of expressing human time, a production or creation of meaning? That is my question.

How would you relate this hermeneutics of narrativity to your former phenomenology of existence?

I would say, borrowing Wittgenstein's term, that the 'language-game' of narration ultimately reveals that the meaning of human existence is itself narrative. The implications of narration as a retelling of history are considerable. For history is not only the story (*histoire*) of triumphant kings and heroes, of the powerful; it is also the story of the powerless and dispossessed. The history of the vanquished dead crying out for justice demands to be told. As Hannah Arendt points out, the meaning of human existence is not just the power to change or master the world, but also the ability to be remembered and recollected in narrative discourse, to be *memorable.* These existential and historical implications of narrativity are very far-reaching, for they determine what is to be 'preserved' and rendered 'permanent' in a culture's sense of its own past, of its own 'identity'.

> Could you outline some such implications for a political rereading of the past? How, for example, would it relate to a Marxist interpretation?

Just as novelists choose a certain plot (*intrigue*) to order the material of their fiction into a narrative sequence, so too historians order the events of the past according to certain choices of narrative structure or plot. While history has traditionally concerned itself with the plot of kings, battles, treaties and the rise and fall of empires, one finds alternative readings emerging from the nineteenth century onwards whose narrative selection focuses on the story of the victims – the plot of suffering rather than that of power and glory. Michelet's romantic historiography of the 'people' was a case in point. And a more obvious and influential example is the Marxist rereading of history according to the model of the class struggle which champions the cause of the oppressed workers. In such ways, the normal narrative ordering of history is reversed and the hero is now the 'slave' rather than the 'master' as before; a new set of events and facts are deemed to be relevant and claim our attention; the relations of labour and production take precedence over the relations between kings and queens. But here again one must remain critical lest the new heroes of history become abstractions in their turn, thus reducing an alternative 'liberating' plot to another reified version of events which might only deepen the illusion that history somehow unfolds of its own accord independently of the creative powers of the labouring human subject. After such a manner, Marxism as an ideology of liberation, of the powerless, can easily become – as happened with the German Social Democrats or with Stalin – an ideology which imposes a new kind of oppressive power: the proletariat thus ceases to be a living human community of subjects and becomes instead an impersonal, abstracted concept in a new system of scientific determinism.

> Is narrative language primarily an intentionality of subjective consciousness, as phenomenology argued; or is it an objective

and impersonal structure which predetermines the subjective operations of consciousness, as structuralism maintained?

It is both at once. The invaluable contribution made by structuralism was to offer an exact scientific description of the codes and paradigms of language. But I do not believe that this excludes the creative expression of consciousness. The creation of meaning in language comes from the specifically *human* production of new ways of expressing the objective paradigms and codes made available by language. With the same grammar, for example, we can utter many novel and different sentences. Creativity is always governed by objective linguistic codes which it continually brings to their limit in order to invent something new. Whereas I drew from the objective codes of rhetoric in my analysis of the creative power of metaphor, in my study of narrativity I refer to the linguistic structures disclosed by the Russian formalists, the Prague school and more recently by the structuralism of Lévi-Strauss and Genette. My philosophical project is to show how human language is *inventive* despite the objective limits and codes which govern it, to reveal the diversity and potentiality of language which the erosion of the everyday, conditioned by technocratic and political interests, never ceases to obscure. To become aware of the metaphorical and narrative resources of language is to recognize that its flattened or diminished powers can always be rejuvenated for the benefit of all forms of language usage.

Can your research on narrativity also be considered as a search for a shared meaning beyond the multiplicity of discourses? In other words, does the act of narrating history render it universal and common to all men?

This problem of unity and diversity is central to narrativity and can be summarized in terms of the two following, conflicting interpretations. In the *Confessions* Augustine tells us that the 'human body is undone', that human existence is in discord in so far as it is a temporal rupturing and exploding of the present in contrast to the eternal presence of God. To this Augustinian reading of human existence as *dispersion*, I would oppose Aristotle's theory of tragedy in *The Poetics* as a way of *unifying* existence by retelling it. Narrativity can be seen in terms of this opposition: the discordance of time (*temps*) and the concordance of the tale (*récit*). This is a problem which faces all historians, for example. Is history a narrative tale which orders and constructs the fragmentary, empirical facts offered by sociology? Can history divorce itself from the narrative structure of the tale, in its rapprochement to sociology, without ceasing to be history? It is interesting that even Fernand Braudel, who champions the sociological approach to history in his preface to *The Mediterranean in the Time of Philippe II*, still retains the notion of history as temporal duration; he stops short of espousing atemporal paradigms, *à la* Lévi-Strauss, for that would spell the demise of history. Lévi-Strauss's social anthropology can afford to dispense with history since it is only concerned with 'cold societies': societies without historical or diachronic development, whose customs and norms – the incest taboo, for example – are largely unaffected by temporal change. History begins and ends with the reciting of a tale (*récit*); and its intelligibility and coherence rest upon this recital. My task is to show how the narrative structures of history and of the story (i.e. of the novel or fiction) operate in a parallel fashion to create new forms of human time, and therefore new forms of human community, for creativity is also a social and cultural act; it is not confined to the individual.

What exactly do you mean by 'human' time?

I mean the formulation of two opposing forms of time: public time and private time. Private time is mortal time, for, as Heidegger says, to exist is to be a being-towards-death (*Sein-zum-Tode*), a being whose future is closed off by death. As soon as we understand our existence as this mortal time, we are already involved in a form of private narrativity or history; as soon as the individual comes up against the finite limits of its own existence, it is obliged to recollect itself and to make time its *own*. On the other hand, there exists public time. Now I do not mean public in the sense of physical or natural time (clock time), but the time of language itself, which continues on after the individual's death. To live in human time is to live between the private time of our mortality and the public time of language. Even Chénu, who tends towards a quantitative assessment of history, acknowledges that the kernel of history is demography, that is, the regeneration of generations, the story (*histoire*) of the living and the dead. Precisely as this recollection of the living and the dead, history – as public narrativity – produces human time. To summarize, I would say that my analysis of narrativity is concerned with three interrelated problems:

(i) narration as history; (ii) narration as fiction; and (iii) narration as human time.

> What can this analysis contribute to your study of the biblical patterns of narration in *La Symbolique du mal*?

The hermeneutics of narration is crucial to our understanding of the Bible. Why is it, for example, that Judeo-Christianity is founded on narrative episodes or stories?; and how is it that these succeed in becoming *exemplary*, co-ordinated into laws, prophecies and psalms, etc.? I think that the biblical co-ordination of narratives can perhaps best be understood in terms of Kristeva's notion of *inter-textuality*: the idea that every text functions in terms of another. Biblical narratives operate in terms of other prescriptive texts. The kernel of biblical hermeneutics is this conjunction of narrativity and prescription.

> What is the rapport between your earlier analysis of the 'creative imagination' as an 'eschatological hope' for the 'not yet' of history, and your more recent analysis of narrativity as the production of human time and history?

Whereas the analysis of creative imagination dealt with creativity in its prospective or futural aspect, the analysis of narrativity deals with it in a retrospective fashion. Fiction has a strong relation to the past. Camus' *L'Étranger*, like most other novels, is written in the passive tense. The narrative voice of a novel generally retells something that has taken place in a fictional past. One could almost say that fictional narration tends to suspend the eschatological in order to inscribe us in a meaningful past. And I believe that we must have a sense of the meaningfulness of the past if our projections into the future are to be more than empty utopias. Heidegger argues in *Being and Time* that it is because we are turned towards the future that we can possess and repossess a past, both our personal past and our cultural heritage. The structure of narrativity demonstrates that it is by trying to put order on our past, by retelling and recounting what has been, that we acquire an identity. These two orientations – towards the future and towards the past – are not, however, incompatible. As Heidegger himself points out, the notion of 'repeating' (*Wiederholung*) the past is inseparable from the existential projection of ourselves towards our possibilities. To 'repeat' our story, to retell our history, is to re-collect our horizon of possibilities in a resolute and responsible manner. In this respect, one can see how the retrospective character of narration is closely linked to the prospective horizon of the future. To say that narration is a recital which orders the past is not to imply that it is a conservative closure to what is new. On the contrary, narration preserves the meaning that is behind us so that we can have meaning before us. There is always *more* order in what we narrate than in what we have actually already lived; and this narrative excess (*surcroît*) of order, coherence and unity, is a prime example of the creative power of narration.

> What about the modernist texts of Joyce and Beckett, etc., where the narrative seems to disperse and dislocate meaning?

These texts break up the habitual paradigms of narrative order in order to leave the ordering task of creation to the reader himself. And ultimately it is true that the reader composes the text. All narrative, however, even Joyce's, is a certain call to order. Joyce does not invite us to embrace chaos but an infinitely more complex order. Narrative carries us beyond the oppressive order of our existence to a more liberating and refined order. The question of narrativity, no matter how modernist or avant-garde, cannot be separated from the problem of order.

> What compelled you to abandon the Husserlian phenomenology of consciousness, with its claim to a direct and immediate apprehension of meaning, and to adopt a hermeneutic phenomenology where the meaning of existence is approached indirectly through myth, metaphor or narrativity, that is, through the detour of mediation?

I think that it is always through the mediation of structuring operations that one apprehends the fundamental meaning of existence, what Merleau-Ponty called *l'être sauvage*. Merleau-Ponty sought this *l'être sauvage* throughout his philosophical career and consistently criticized its deformation and obfuscation in science. I for my part have always attempted to identify those mediations of language which are not reducible to the dissimulations of scientific objectivity, but which continue to bear witness to creative linguistic potentialities. Language possesses deep resources which are not immediately reducible to knowledge (particularly the intellectualist and behaviourist forms of knowledge which Merleau-Ponty rejected). And my interest in hermeneutics, and its interpretation of language which extends to the limits of logic and the mathematical sciences, has always been an attempt to detect and describe these resources. I am convinced that all figurative language is potentially conceptualizable and that the conceptual order can possess a form of creativity. This is why I insisted, at the end of *La Métaphore vive*, upon the essential connection or intersection between speculative and poetic discourse – evidenced, for example, in the whole question of analogy. It is simplistic to suggest that conceptualization is *per se* anatagonistic to the meaning of life and experience; concepts can also be open, creative and living, though they can never constitute a knowledge which would be immediately accessible to some self-transparent *cogito*. Conceptualization cannot reach meaning directly or create meaning out of itself *ex nihilo*; it cannot dispense with the detour of mediation through figurative structures. This detour is intrinsic to the very working of concepts.

> In study 8 of *La Métaphore vive* you raised the complex philosophical problem of 'reference' in language. How does narrativity relate to this problem of reference?

This question brings us to the intersection between history, which claims to deal with what actually happens, and the novel, which is of the order of fiction. Reference entails a conjunction of history and fiction. And I reckon that my chances of demonstrating the validity of reference are better in an analysis of narrativity than in one of metaphoricity. Whereas it is always difficult to identify the referent of poetic or metaphorical discourse, the referent of narrative discourse is obvious – the order of human action. Now of course human action itself is charged with fictional entities such as stories, symbols, rites, etc. As Marx pointed out in *The German Ideology*, when men produce their existence in the form of *praxis* they represent it to themselves in terms of fiction, even at the limit in terms of religion (which for Marx is the model of ideology). There can be no praxis which is not already symbolically structured in some way. Human action is always figured in signs, interpreted in terms of cultural traditions and norms. Our narrative fictions are then added to this primary interpretation or figuration of human action; so that narrative is a redefining of what is already defined, a reinterpretation of what is already interpreted. The referent of narration, namely human action, is never raw or immediate reality but an action which has been symbolized and resymbolized over and over again. Thus narration serves to displace anterior symbolizations on to a new plane, integrating or exploding them as the case may be. If this were not so, if literary narrative, for example, were closed off from the world of human action, it would be entirely harmless and inoffensive. But literature never ceases to challenge our way of reading human history and praxis. In this respect, literary narrative involves a creative use of language often ignored by science or by our everyday existence. Literary language has the capacity to put our quotidian existence into question; it is *dangerous* in the best sense of the word.

> But is not the hermeneutic search for mediated and symbolized meaning a way of escaping from the harsh, empirical reality of things, is it not always working at one remove from life?

Proust said that if play was cloistered off in books, it would cease to be formidable. Play is formidable precisely because it is loose in the world, planting its mediations everywhere, shattering the illusion of the immediacy of the real. The problem for a hermeneutics of language is not to rediscover some pristine immediacy but to mediate again and again in a new and more creative fashion. The mediating role of imagination is forever at work in lived reality (*le vécu*). There is no lived reality, no human or social reality, which is not already *represented* in some sense. This imaginative and creative dimension of the social, this *imaginaire social*, has been brilliantly analysed by Castoriadis in his book, *L'Institution imaginaire de la société*. Literature supplements this primary representation of the social with its own narrative representation, a process which Dagonier calls 'iconographic augmentation'. But literature is not the only way in which fiction can iconographically mediate human reality. There is also the mediating role of models in science or of utopias in political ideologies. These three modes of fictional mediation – literary, scientific and political – effectuate a metaphorization of the real, a creation of new meaning.

> Which returns us to your original question: what is the meaning of creativity in language and how does it relate to the codes, structures or laws imposed by language?

Linguistic creativity constantly strains and stretches the laws and codes of language that regulate it. Roland Barthes described these regulating laws as 'fascist' and urged the writer and critic to work at the limits of language, subverting its constraining laws, in order to make way for the free movement of *desire*, to make language festive. But if the narrative order of language is replete with codes, it is also capable of creatively violating them. Human creativity is always in some sense a response to a regulating order. The imagination is always working on the basis of already established laws and it is its task to make them function creatively, either by applying them in an original way or by subverting them; or indeed both – what Malraux calls 'regulated deformation'. There is no function of imagination, no *imaginaire*, that is not structuring or structured, that is not said or about-to-be-said in language. The task of hermeneutics is to charter the unexplored resources of the to-be-said on the basis of the already-said. Imagination never resides in the unsaid.

How would you respond to Lévi-Strauss's conclusion, in *L'Homme nu*, that the structures and symbols of society originate in 'nothing' (*rien*)?

I am not very interested in Lévi-Strauss's metaphysics of nothingness. The great contribution made by Lévi-Strauss was to identify the existence of enduring symbolic structures in what he called 'cold societies', that is, societies (mainly South-American Indian) resistant to historical change. The Greek and Hebraic societies which combined to make up our Western culture are, by contrast, 'hot societies'; they are societies whose symbolic systems change and evolve over time, carrying within themselves different layers of interpretation and reinterpretation. In other words, in 'hot' societies the work of interpretation is not – as in 'cold' societies – something which is introduced from without, but an internal component of the symbolic system itself. It is precisely this diachronic process of reinterpretation that we call 'tradition'. In the Greek *Iliad*, for example, we discover a myth that is already reinterpreted, a piece of history that is already reworked into a narrative order. Neither Homer nor Aeschylus invented their stories; what they did invent were new narrative meanings, new forms of retelling the same story. The author of the *Iliad* has the entire story of the Trojan War at his disposal, but chooses to isolate the exemplary story of Achilles' wrath. He develops this exemplary narrative to the point where the wrath expires in the cathartic reconciliation – occasioned by Hector's death – with King Priam. The story produces and exemplifies a particular meaning: how the vain and meaningless wrath of one hero (Achilles) can be overcome when this hero becomes reconciled with his victim's father (Priam) at the funeral banquet. Here we have a powerful example of what it means to create meaning from a common mythic heritage, to receive a tradition and re-create it poetically to signify something new.

> And of course Chaucer and Shakespeare produced different 'exemplary' reinterpretations of the *Iliad* myth in their respective versions of Troilus and Cressida; as did Joyce once again in *Ulysses*. Such reinterpretation would seem to typify the cultural history of our Hellenic heritage. Is this kind of historical reinterpretation also to be found in the biblical or Hebraic tradition?

Yes, the biblical narratives of the Hebraic tradition also operate in this *exemplary* or exemplifying fashion. This is evident in the fact that the biblical stories or episodes are not simply added to each other, or juxtaposed with each other, but constitute a cumulative and organic development. For example, the promise made to Abraham that his people would have a salvific relation with God is an inexhaustible promise (unlike certain legal promises which can be immediately realized); as such it opens up a history in which this promise can be repeated and reinterpreted over and over again – with Moses, then with David, and so on. So that the biblical narrative of this 'not yet realized' promise creates a cumulative history of repetition. The Christian message of crucifixion and resurrection then inserts itself into this biblical history, as a double rapport of reinterpretation and rupture. Christianity plays both a subversive and preservative role *vis-à-vis* the Judaic tradition. Saint Paul talks about the overcoming of the Law; and yet we find the synoptic authors continually affirming that the Christian event is a response to the prophetic promise, 'according to the Scriptures'. The Judaic and Christian reinterpretations of biblical history are in 'loving combat', to borrow Jaspers' phrase. The important point is that the biblical experience of faith is founded on stories and narratives – the story of the exodus, the crucifixion and resurrection, etc. – *before* it expresses itself in abstract theologies which interpret these foundational narratives and provide religious tradition with its sense of enduring identity. The *future* projects of every religion are intimately related to the ways in which it remembers itself.

> Your work in hermeneutics always displays a particular sensitivity to this 'conflict of interpretations' – even to the point of providing one of the titles of your books. Your hermeneutics has consistently refused the idea of an 'absolute knowledge' which might reductively *totalize* the multiplicity of interpretations – phenomenological, theological, psychoanalytic, structuralist, scientific, literary, etc. Is there any sense in which this open-ended intellectual itinerary can be construed as a sort of odyssey which might ultimately return to a unifying centre where the conflicting interpretations of human discourse could be gathered together and reconciled?

When Odysseus completes the circle and returns to his island of Ithaca there is slaughter and destruction. For me the philosophical task is not to close the circle, to centralize or totalize knowledge, but to keep open the irreducible plurality of discourse. It is essential to show how the different discourses may interrelate or intersect but one must resist the temptation to make them identical, the same. My departure from Husserlian phenomenology was largely due to my disagreement with its theory of a controlling transcendental *cogito*. I advanced the notion of a wounded or split *cogito*, in opposition to the idealist claims for an inviolate absolute subjectivity. It was in fact Karl Barth who first taught me that the subject is not a centralizing master but rather a disciple or auditor of a language larger than itself. At a broader cultural level, we must also be wary of attending exclusively to *Western* traditions of thought, of becoming *Europocentric*. In emphasizing the importance of the Greek or Judeo-Christian traditions, we often overlook the radically heterogeneous discourses of the Far East for example. One of my American colleagues recently suggested to me that Derrida's deconstruction of logocentrism bears striking resemblances to the Buddhist notion of nothingness. I think that there is a certain 'degree zero' or emptiness which we may have to traverse in order to abandon our pretension to be the centre, our tendency to reduce all other discourses to our own totalizing schemas of thought. If there is an ultimate unity, it resides elsewhere, in a sort of eschatological hope. But this is my 'secret', if you wish, my personal wager, and not something that can be translated into a centralizing philosophical discourse.

> It appears that our modern secularized society has abandoned the symbolic representations or *imaginaire* of tradition. Can the creative process of reinterpretation operate if the narrative continuity with the past is broken?

A society where narrative is dead is one where men are no longer capable of exchanging their experiences, of sharing a common experience. The contemporary search for some narrative continuity with the past is not just nostalgic escapism but a contestation of the legislative and planificatory discourse which tends to predominate in bureaucratic societies. To give people back a *memory* is also to give them back a *future*, to put them back in time and thus release them from the 'instantaneous mind' (*mens instans*), to borrow a term from Leibniz. The past is not *passé*, for our future is guaranteed precisely by our ability to possess a narrative identity, to recollect the past in historical or fictive form. This problem of narrative identity is particularly acute, for instance, in a country like France, where the Revolution represented a rupture with the patrimony of legend and folklore, etc. (I have always been struck, for example, by the fact that most of the so-called 'traditional' songs the French still possess are drinking songs.) Today the French are largely bereft of a shared *imaginaire*, a common symbolic heritage. Our task then is to reappropriate those resources of language which have resisted contamination and destruction. To rework language is to rediscover what we are. What is lost in experience is often salvaged in language, sedimented as a deposit of traces, as a thesaurus. There can be no pure or perfectly transparent model of language, as Wittgenstein reminds us in his *Philosophical Investigations*; and if there were it would be no more than a universalized *vide*. To rediscover meaning we must return to the multi-layered sedimentations of language, to the complex plurality of its instances, which can preserve what is said from the destruction of oblivion.

> In *History and Truth* you praise Emmanuel Mounier as someone who refused to separate the search for philosophical truth from a political pedagogy. What are the political implications, if any, of your own philosophical thinking?

My work to date has been a hermeneutic reflection upon the mediation of meaning in language, and particularly in poetic or narrative language. What you ask, can such hermeneutics contribute to our understanding of the rapport between the mediations of such symbolic discourses and the immediacy of political praxis? The fact that language is disclosed by hermeneutics (and also by the analytic philosophy of Wittgenstein) as a non-totalizable plurality of interpretations or 'language-games' means that the rhetorical discourse of politics, which serves as a justification or critique of power, is but one among many other 'language-games' and so cannot pretend to the status of a universal science. Some recent exchanges I had with Czech philosophers and students in the Tomin seminar in Prague taught me that the problem of totalitarianism resides in the lie that there can be a universally true and scientific discourse of politics (in this instance, the communist discourse). Once one recognizes that political language is basically a rhetoric of persuasion and opinion, one can tolerate free discussion. An 'open society', to use Popper's term, is one which acknowledges that political debate is infinitely open and is thus prepared to take the critical step back in order to continually interrogate and reconstitute the conditions of an authentic language.

Can there be a positive rapport between language, as political ideology, and utopia?

Every society, as I mentioned earlier, possesses, or is part of, a socio-political *imaginaire*, that is, an ensemble of symbolic discourses. This *imaginaire* can function as a rupture or a reaffirmation. As reaffirmation, the *imaginaire* operates as an '*ideology*' which can positively repeat and represent the founding discourse of a society, what I call its 'foundational symbols', thus preserving its sense of identity. After all, cultures create themselves by telling stories of their own past. The danger is of course that this reaffirmation can be perverted, usually by monopolistic elites, into a mystificatory discourse which serves to uncritically vindicate or glorify the established political powers. In such instances, the symbols of a community become fixed and fetishized; they serve as lies. Over against this, there exists the *imaginaire* of rupture, a discourse of *utopia* which remains critical of the powers that be out of fidelity to an 'elsewhere', to a society that is 'not yet'. But this utopian discourse is not always positive either. For besides the authentic utopia of critical rupture there can also exist a dangerously schizophrenic utopian discourse which projects a static future without ever producing the conditions of its realization. This can happen with the Marxist–Leninist notion of utopia if one projects the final 'withering away of the State' without undertaking genuine measures to ever achieve such a goal. Here utopia becomes a future cut off from the present and the past, a mere alibi for the consolidation of the repressive powers that be. The utopian discourse functions as a mystificatory ideology as soon as it justifies the oppression of today in the name of the liberation of tomorrow. In short, *ideology* as a symbolic confirmation of the past and *utopia* as a symbolic opening towards the future are complementary; if cut off from each other then can lead to a form of political pathology.

Would you consider the Liberation Theology of Latin America to be an example of a positive utopian discourse in so far as it combines a Marxist utopianism with the political transformation of *present* reality?

It also combines it with the *past*, with the memory of the archetypes of exodus and resurrection. This memorial dimension of Liberation Theology is essential, for it gives direction and continuity to the utopian projection of the future, thus functioning as a *garde-fou* against irresponsible or uncritical futurism. Here the political project of the future is inseparable from a continuous horizon of liberation, reaching back to the biblical notions of exile and promise. The promise remains unfulfilled until the utopia is historically realized; and it is precisely the not-yet-realized horizon of this promise which binds men together as a community, which prevents utopia detaching itself as an empty dream.

How exactly does utopia relate to history?

In his *History of the Concept of History*, Reinhart Kosselek argues that until the eighteenth century, the concept of history, in the West at any rate, was a plural one; one referred to 'histories' not History with a capital H. Our current notion of a single or unique history only emerged with the modern idea of progress. As soon as history is thus constituted as a single concept, the gap between our 'horizon of expectancy' and our 'field of experience' never ceases to widen. The unity of history is founded on the constitution of a common horizon of expectancy; but the projection of such a horizon into a distantly abstract future means that our present 'field of experience' can become pathologically deprived of meaning and articulation. The universal ceases to be concrete. This dissociation of *expectancy* from *experience* enters a crisis as soon as we lack the intermediaries to pass from the one to the other. Up to the sixteenth century, the utopian horizon of expectancy was the eschatological notion of the Last Judgment, which had as mediating or intermediating factors the whole experience of the millenium of the Holy Roman and Germanic Empires. There was always some sort of articulated path leading from what one had to what one expected to have. The liberal ideology of Kant and Locke produced a certain discourse of democracy which served as a path for the citizen towards a better humanity; and Marxism also promoted mediating stages leading from capitalism through socialism to communism. But we don't seem to believe in these intermediaries any more. The problem today is the apparent impossibility of unifying world politics, of mediating between the polycentricity of our everyday political practice and the utopian horizon of a universally liberated humanity. It is not that we are without utopia, but that we are without *paths* to utopia. And without a path towards it, without concrete and practical mediation in our field of experience, utopia becomes a sickness. Perhaps the deflation of utopian expectancies is not entirely a bad thing. Politics can so easily be injected with too much utopia; perhaps it should become more modest and realistic in its claims, more committed to our practical and immediate needs.

Is there any place in contemporary politics for a genuine utopian discourse?

Maybe not in politics itself but rather at the junction between politics and other cultural discourses. Our present disillusionment with the political stems from the fact that we invested it with the totality of our expectancies – until it became a bloated imposture of utopia. We have tended to forget that beside the public realm of politics, there also exists a more private cultural realm (which includes literature, philosophy and religion, etc.) where the utopian horizon can express itself. Modern society seems hostile to this domain of private experience, but the suppression of the private entails the destruction of the public. The vanquishing of the private by the public is a pyrrhic victory.

Are you advocating a return to the bourgeois romantic notion of private subjectivity removed from all political responsibility?

Not at all. In my recent discussions with the Prague philosophers I spoke about the crisis of the subject in contemporary Continental philosophy, particularly structuralism. I pointed out that if one does away with the idea of a subject who is responsible for his or her words, we are no longer in a position to talk of the freedom or the rights of man. To dispense with the classical notion of the subject as a transparent *cogito* does not mean that we have to dispense with all forms of subjectivity. My hermeneutical philosophy has attempted to demonstrate the existence of an opaque subjectivity which expresses itself through the detour of countless mediations – signs, symbols, texts and human praxis itself. This hermeneutical idea of subjectivity as a dialectic between the self and mediated social meanings has deep moral and political implications. It shows that there is an *ethic of the word*, that language is not just the abstract concern of logic or semiotics, but entails the fundamental moral duty that people be responsible for what they say. A society which no longer possesses subjects ethically responsible for their words is a society which no longer possesses citizens. For the dissident philosophers in Prague the primary philosophical question is the integrity and truthfulness of language. And this question becomes a moral and political act of resistance in a system based on lies and perversion. The Marxism of Eastern Europe has degenerated from dialectics to positivism. It has abandoned the Hegelian inspiration which preserved Marxism as a realization of the universal subject in history, and has become instead a positivistic technology of mass manipulation.

So the hermeneutical interrogation of the creation of meaning in language can have a political content?

Perhaps the most promising example of a political hermeneutics is to be found in the Frankfurt School synthesis between Marxist dialectics and Heideggerian hermeneutics – best expressed in Habermas' critique of ideologies. But here again one must be careful to resist the temptation to engage in an unmediated politics. It is necessary for hermeneutics to keep a certain distance so as to critically disclose the underlying mediating structures at work in political discourse. This hermeneutic distance is particularly important today with the post-1968 disillusionment, the demise of the Maoist ideology and the exposure of Soviet totalitarianism by Solzhenitsyn and others.

Is this disillusionment a world-wide phenomenon?

It exists in varying degrees, but is most conspicuous in countries like France where the essential distinction between state and society has been largely occluded. The French Revolution apportioned political sovereignty to all levels of the community, from the government at the top to the individuals at the bottom. But in this process, the state became omnipresent, the citizen being reduced to a mere fragment of the state. What was so striking in the Solidarity movement in Poland was their use of the term 'society' in opposition to the term 'state'. Even in the Anglo-Saxon countries one finds certain national institutions – such as the media or universities – which are relatively independent of state politics. (It is difficult to find examples of this in France.) The weak ideologization of politics in America, for instance, means that it can at least serve as a sprawling laboratory where a multiplicity of discourses can be tried and tested. This phenomenon of the 'melting pot' is an example of what Montesquieu called the 'separation of powers'. It is interesting to remember that the state was originally conceived by the liberal thinkers as an agency of toleration, a way of protecting the plurality of beliefs and practices. The liberal state was to be a safeguard against religious and other forms of fanaticism. The fundamental perversion of the liberal state is that it came to function as a totalizing rather than a detotalizing agency. That is why it is urgent for us today to discover a political discourse which would not be governed by states, a new form of society guaranteeing universal rights yet dispensing with totalizing constraints. This is the enormous task of reconstituting a form of sociality not determined by the state.

How does one go about discovering this new discourse of society?

One of the first steps would be to analyse what exactly happened in the eighteenth century when the Judeo-Christian horizon of eschatology was replaced by the Enlightenment horizon of humanism with its liberal notions of autonomy, freedom and human rights. We must see how this Enlightenment humanism developed through the Kantian notion of the autonomous will, the Hegelian notion of the universal class (of civil servants) to the Marxist universal class of workers, etc. until we reached a secularized version of utopia which frequently degenerated into scientific positivism. We must ask: can there be any sort of continuity between the religious–eschatological projection of utopia and the modern humanist projection of a secularized utopia? The challenge today is to find alternative forms of social rationality beyond the positivistic extremes of both state socialism and utilitarian–liberal capitalism. Habermas' distinction between three forms of rationality is essential here: (i) *calculative rationality*, which operates as positivistic control and manipulation; (ii) *interpretative rationality*, which tries to represent the cultural codes and norms in a creative way; (iii) *critical rationality*, which opens up the utopian horizon of liberation. For a genuine social rationality to exist we must refuse to allow the critical and interpretative functions to be reduced to the calculative. Habermas is here developing Adorno's and Horkheimer's critique of *positivist rationality*, which exists in both state communism and in the argument of liberal capitalism that once the society of abundance has been achieved all can be distributed equally (the problem being, of course, that liberalism employs the means of an hierarchical and unequal society to achieve such an end of abundance – an end which never seems to be realized). So our task remains that of preserving a utopian horizon of liberty and equality – by means of interpretative and critical rationality – without resorting to a positivistic ideology of bad faith. I agree here with Raymond Aron's contention that we have not yet succeeded in developing a political model which could accommodate the simultaneous advancement of liberty and equality. Societies which have advocated liberty have generally suppressed equality and vice versa.

> Do you think that the critique of political power carried out by left-wing political philosophers in France, such as Castoriadis and Lefort, contributes to the hermeneutic search for a new discourse of sociality?

Their contribution has been absolutely decisive. This critique has attempted to show that the error of Marxism resides not so much in its lack of a political horizon as in its reduction of the critique of power to the economic transfer of work to capital (that is, the critique of surplus value). Thus the Marxist critique tends to ignore that there can be more pernicious forms of power than capital – for example, the totalization of all the resources of a society (the resources of the workforce, of the means of discussion and information, education, research, etc.) by the central committee of the party or state. In this manner the handing over of the private ownership of the means of production to the state can often mean a replacement of the alienation of society by the alienation of the state. The power of the totalitarian party is perhaps more nefarious than the dehumanizing power of capital in so far as it controls not only the economic means of production but also the political means of communications. Maybe the economic analysis of class struggle is but one of the many plots that make up the complex of history. Hence the need for a hermeneutics of sociality that could unravel the plurality of power plots which enmesh to form our history.

> In 'Non-violent Man and his Presence in History' (*History and Truth*) you asked: 'Can the prophet or non-violent man have an historical task which would obviate both the extreme inefficacity of the Yogi and the extreme efficacity of the Commissar?' In other words, can one commit oneself to the efficacious transformation of political reality and still preserve the critical distance of transcendence?

This idea of transcendence is essential for any sort of non-violent discourse. The pacifist ideal resists violence by attesting to values which transcend the arena of political efficacity, without becoming irrelevant dreams. Non-violence is a form of genuine utopian vigil or hope, a way of refuting the system of violence and oppression in which we live.

> Is it possible to reconcile the exigency of an authentic social rationality with the eschatological hope of religion?

This has never struck me as an insoluble problem for the basic cultural reason that our Western religiosity of Judeo-Christianity has always functioned in the philosophical climate of Greek and Latin rationality. I have always objected to the simplistic opposition of Jerusalem and Athens, to those thinkers who declare that true spirituality can only be found in monotheism; or try to drive a wedge between Greek and Hebraic culture, defining the former as a thought of the cosmos and the latter as a thought of transcendence, etc. From the eleventh century onwards we find models for reconciling reason and religion – in Anselm, for example – and the Renaissance confirms this primary synthesis of rationality and spirituality. If it is true that the rationality of scientific positivism has divorced itself from spirituality, there are many signs today that we are searching for new forms of connection.

II: Myth as the bearer of possible worlds★

> One of your first attempts at hermeneutic analysis concentrated on the way in which human consciousness was mediated by mythic and symbolic expressions from the earliest times. In *The Symbolism of Evil* (1960) you demonstrated how mythic symbols played an important ideological and political role in the ancient cultures of the Babylonians, Hebrews and Greeks, etc. And in this same work you declared that 'myth relates to events that happened at the beginning of time which have the purpose of providing grounds for the ritual actions of men of today' (p. 5). Are you suggesting that mythic symbols can play a relevant role in contemporary culture? And if so, could you elaborate on how it might do so?

I don't think that we can approach this question directly, that is, in terms of a direct relationship between myth and action. We must first return to an analysis of what constitutes the *imaginary nucleus* of any culture. It is my conviction that one cannot reduce any culture to its explicit functions – political, economic and legal, etc. No culture is wholly transparent in this way. There is invariably a hidden nucleus which determines and rules the *distribution* of these transparent functions and institutions. It is this matrix of distribution which assigns them different roles in relation to (1) each other, (2) other societies, (3) the individuals who participate in them, and (4) nature, which stands over against them.

> Does this ratio of distribution differ from one society to another?

★A shortened version of this dialogue appeared in *The Crane Bag Journal of Irish Studies* (edited by Richard Kearney and Mark Hederman), vol. 2, nos 1 and 2, 1978.

It certainly does. The particular relationship between political institutions, nature and the individual is rarely if ever the same in any two cultures. The ratio of distribution between these different functions of a given society is determined by some *hidden* nucleus, and it is here that we must situate the specific identity of culture. Beyond or beneath the self-understanding of a society there is an opaque kernel which cannot be reduced to empirical norms or laws. This kernel cannot be explained in terms of some transparent model because it is constitutive of a culture *before* it can be expressed and reflected in specific representations or ideas. It is only if we try to grasp this kernel that we may discover the *foundational mytho-poetic* nucleus of a society. By analysing itself in terms of such a foundational nucleus, a society comes to a truer understanding of itself; it begins to critically acknowledge its own symbolizing identity.

How are we to recognize this mythical nucleus?

The mythical nucleus of a society is only *indirectly* recognizable. But it is indirectly recognizable not only by what is said (discourse), but also by what and how one lives (praxis), and thirdly, as I suggested, by the distribution between different functional levels of a society. We cannot, for example, say that in all countries the economic layer is determining. This is true for our Western society. But as Lévi-Strauss has shown in his analysis of many primitive societies, this is not universally true. In several cultures the significance of economic and historical considerations would seem to be minor. In our culture the economic factor is indeed determining; but that does not mean that the predominance of economics is itself explicable purely in terms of economic science. This predominance is perhaps more correctly understood as but one constituent of the overall evaluation of what is primary and what is secondary. And it is only by the analysis of the hierarchical structuring and evaluation of the different constituents of a society (i.e. the role of politics, nature, art, religion, etc.) that we may penetrate to its hidden *mytho-poetic nucleus*.

You mentioned Lévi-Strauss. How would you situate your own hermeneutical analyses of symbol and myth in relation to his work in this area?

I don't think that Lévi-Strauss makes any claim to speak of societies in general. He has focused on certain primitive and stable societies, leaving aside considerations of history. This is important to realize so as not to draw hasty conclusions from his analyses. Lévi-Strauss has deliberately chosen to speak of societies *without history*, whereas I think that there is something specifically historical about the societies to which we in the West belong, depending on the extent to which they are affected by Hebraic, Hellenic, Germanic or Celtic cultures. The development of a society is both synchronic and diachronic. This means that the distribution of power-functions in any given society contains a definite *historical* dimension. We have to think of societies in terms of both a set of simultaneous institutions (synchronism) and a process of historical transformation (diachronism). Thus we arrive at the panchronic approach to societies, i.e. both synchronic and diachronic, which characterises the hermeneutical method. And we must also realize that the kinds of myth on which our societies are founded have themselves this twofold characteristic: on the one hand, they constitute a certain system of simultaneous symbols which can be approached through structuralist analysis; but, on the other hand, they have a history, because it is always through a process of interpretation and reinterpretation that they are kept alive. Myths have a historicity of their own. This difference of history typifies, for example, the development of the Semitic, pre-Hellenistic and Celtic mythical nuclei. Therefore, just as societies are both structural and historical, so also are the mythical nuclei which ground them.

> In the conclusion to *The Symbolism of Evil* you state that 'a philosophy instructed by myths arises at a certain moment in reflection and wishes to answer to a certain situation in modern culture'. What precisely do you mean by this 'certain situation'? And how does myth answer to this problematic?

I was thinking there of Jaspers' philosophy of 'boundary situations', which influenced me so strongly just after the Second World War. There are certain boundary situations such as war, suffering, guilt, death, etc. in which the individual or community experiences a fundamental existential crisis. At such moments the whole community is put into question. For it is only when it is threatened with destruction from without or from within that a society is compelled to return to the very roots of its identity; to that mythical nucleus which ultimately grounds and determines it. The solution to the immediate crisis is no longer a purely political or technical matter but demands that we ask ourselves the ultimate questions concerning our origins and ends: Where do we come from? Where do we go? In this way, we become aware of our basic capacities and reasons for surviving, for being and continuing to be what we are.

I am reminded here of Mircea Eliade's statement in *Myths, Dreams, Mysteries* that myth is something which always operates in a society regardless of whether this society reflectively acknowledges its existence. Eliade maintains that because modern man has lost his awareness of the important role that myth plays in his life, it often manifests itself in *deviant* ways. He gives as an example the emergence of fascist movements in Europe characterized by a mythic glorification of blood sacrifice and the hero-saviour together with the equally mythical revival of certain ancient rituals, symbols and insignia. The suggestion is that if we do not explicitly recognize and reappropriate the mythic import of our existence it will emerge in distorted and pernicious ways. Do you think this is a valid point?

You have hit here on a very important and difficult problem: the possibilities of a perversion of myth. This means that we can no longer approach myth *at the level of naivety*. We must rather always view it from a critical perspective. It is only by means of a selective reappropriation that we can become aware of myth. We are no longer primitive beings, living at the immediate level of myth. Myth for us is always mediated and opaque. This is so not only because it expresses itself primarily through a particular apportioning of power-functions, as mentioned earlier, but also because several of its recurrent forms have become deviant and dangerous, e.g. the myth of absolute power (fascism) and the myth of the sacrificial scapegoat (anti-Semitism and racism). We are no longer justified in speaking of 'myth in general'. We must critically assess the content of each myth and the basic intentions which animate it. Modern man can neither get rid of myth nor take it at its face value. Myth will always be with us, but we must always approach it *critically*.

It was with a similar scruple in mind that I tried to show in *Myth and Terror* (1978) that there are certain mythic structures operative in extreme Irish Republicanism – recurrence of

> blood sacrifice, apocalypse/renewal, etc. – which can become deviant manifestations of an original mythical nucleus. And I feel accordingly that any approach to myth should be as much a demythologization of deviant expressions as a resuscitation of genuine ones.

Yes. And I think it is here that we could speak of the essential connection between the 'critical instance' and the 'mythical foundation'. Only those myths are genuine which can be reinterpreted in terms of *liberation*. And I mean liberation as both a personal and collective phenomenon. We should perhaps sharpen this critical criterion to include only those myths which have as their horizon the liberation of mankind *as a whole*. Liberation cannot be exclusive. Here I think we come to recognize a fundamental convergence between the claims of myth and reason. In genuine reason as in genuine myth we find a concern for the *universal* liberation of men. To the extent that myth is seen as the foundation of a particular community to the absolute exclusion of all others, the possibilities of perversion – chauvenistic nationalism, racism, etc. – are already present.

> So in fact you suggest that the foundational power of myth should always be in some sense chaperoned by critical reason?

In our Western culture the myth-making of man has often been linked with the critical instance of reason. And this is because it has had to be constantly interpreted and reinterpreted in different historical epochs. In other words, it is because the survival of myth calls for perpetual historical interpretation that it involves a critical component. Myths are not unchanging and unchanged antiques which are simply delivered out of the past in some naked, original state. Their specific identity depends on the way in which each generation receives or interprets them according to their needs, conventions and ideological motivations. Hence the necessity of critical discrimination between liberating and destructive modes of reinterpretation.

> Could you give an example of such reinterpretation?

Well, if we take the relation of *mythos* and *logos* in the Greek experience, we could say that myth had been absorbed by the *logos*, but never completely so; for the claim of the *logos* to rule over *mythos* is itself a mythical claim. Myth is thereby reinjected into the *logos* and gives a mythical dimension to reason itself. Thus the rational appropriation of myth becomes also a revival of myth. Another example would be the reinterpretative overlap between the mythical paradigms of the Hebraic exodus and the prophetic dimension in Hebrew literature. And then at a second level, this Hebraic *mythos* came down to us through a Hellenization of its whole history. Even for us today, this Hellenization is an important mediation because it was through the conjunction of the Jewish *Torah* and Greek *logos* that the notion of law could be incorporated into our culture.

You would not agree then with those modern theologians, such as Moltmann and Bultmann, who suggest that the Hellenization of the Judeo-Christian culture is a perversion of its original richness?

No. The tension between the Greek *logos* and the Semitic nucleus of exodus and revelation is fundamentally and positively constitutive of our culture.

Several critics have described your hermeneutical approach to myth and symbol as an attempt, almost in the manner of psychoanalysis, to reduce myth to some hidden rational message. In *The Symbolism of Evil* you say that the aim of your philosophy is to disclose through reflection and speculation the *rationality* of symbols (p. 357). And again in *On Interpretation* you state that 'every *mythos* harbours a *logos* which requires to be exhibited' (p. 17). But is it possible to extract the *logos* and yet leave the *mythos* intact? Or is myth something essentially enigmatic and therefore irreducible to rational content?

This criticism must be understood in the following way. There are two uses of the concept of myth. One is myth as the *extension* of a symbolic structure. In this sense it is pointless to speak of a demythologization for that would be tantamount to desymbolization – and this I deny completely. But there is a second sense in which myth serves as an *alienation* of this symbolic structure; here it becomes reified and is misconstrued as an actual materialistic explanation of the world. If we interpret myth *literally*, we misinterpret it. For myth is essentially *symbolic*. It is only in instances of such misinterpretation that we may legitimately speak of demythologization; not concerning its symbolic content but concerning the hardening of its symbolic structures into dogmatic or reified ideologies.

> Do you think that Bultmann's use of the term demythologization had something to do with this confusion between two different types of myth (as creative symbol or reductive ideology)?

Yes I do. Bultmann seems to ignore the complexit, of myth. And so when he speaks, for example, of the necessity to demythologize the myth of the threefold division of the cosmos into Heaven, Earth and Hell, he is treating this myth only in terms of its literal interpretation or rather misinterpretation. But Bultmann does not realize that there is a symbolic as well as a pseudosymbolic or literal dimension in myth, and that demythologization is only valid in relation to this second dimension.

> Are myths *universal*, in terms of their original symbolic structures, or do they originate from *particular* national cultures?

This is a very difficult problem. We are caught here between the claims of two equally valid dimensions of myth. And it is the delicate balance between them that is difficult to find. On the one hand, we must say that mythical structures are not simply universal any more than are languages. Just as man is fragmented between different languages, so also he is fragmented between mythical cycles, each of which is typical of a living culture. We must acknowledge, then, that one of the primary functions of any myth is to found the specific identity of a community. On the other hand, however, we must say that just as languages are in principle translatable one into the other, so too myths have a horizon of universality which allows them to be understood by other cultures. The history of Western culture is made up of a confluence of different myths which have been expatriated from their original community, i.e. Hebrew, Greek, Germanic, Celtic. The horizon of any genuine myth always exceeds the political and geographical boundaries of a specific national or tribal community. Even if we may say that mythical structures *founded* political institutions, they always go beyond the territorial limitations imposed by politics. Nothing travels more extensively and effectively than myth.

Therefore we must conclude that while mythic symbols are rooted in a particular culture, they also have the capacity to emigrate and develop within new cultural frameworks.

Is there not a sense in which perhaps the *source* and not only the historical *transmission* of symbols may be responsible for their universal dimension?

It is quite possible that the supranational quality of myth or symbol may be ultimately traced back to a prehistorical layer from which all particular 'mythical nuclei' might be said to emerge. But it is difficult to determine the nature of this prehistory, for all myths as we know them come down to us through history. Each particular myth has its own history of reinterpretation and emigration. But another possible explanation of the universally common dimension of myth might be that because the myth-making powers of the human imagination are finite, they ensure the frequent recurrence of similar archetypes and motifs.

Certainly the myth of the fall as you analyse it in *The Symbolism of Evil* would seem to be common to many different cultures.

Yes. We could say that genuine myth goes beyond its claim to found a particular community and speaks to man as such. Several exegetes of Jewish literature, for example, have made a distinction between different layers of myth: those which are foundational for the Jewish culture – the 'chronicle dimension'; and those which make up a body of truths valid for all mankind – the 'wisdom dimension'. This seems to me an important distinction and one applicable to other cultures.

In Irish literature over the last 80 years or so one finds a similar distinction between these dimensions. In the Fenian literature of the nineteenth century or the Celtic Twilight literature of Yeats, Lady Gregory and others, myth seems to have been approached as a 'chronicle' of the spiritual origins of the race. For this reason it often strikes one as suffering from a certain hazy occultism and introversion. Joyce, on the other hand, used myth, and particularly the myth of Finn, in its 'wisdom dimension'; that is, as an Irish archetype open to, and capable of assimilating, the rich resources of entirely different cultures. *Finnegans Wake* or *Ulysses* seem to represent an exemplary synthesis of the particular and universal claims of myth.

The important point here is that the original potential of any genuine myth will always transcend the confines of a particular community or nation. The *mythos* of any community is the bearer of something which exceeds its own frontiers; it is the bearer of other *possible* worlds. And I think it is in this horizon of the 'possible' that we discover the *universal* dimensions of symbolic and poetic language:

> You have stated that what animates your philosophical research on symbolism and myth is not 'regret for some sunken atlantis' but 'hope for a re-creation of language' (*The Symbolism of Evil*). What precisely do you mean by this?

Language has lost its original unity. Today it is fragmented not only geographically into different communities but functionally into different disciplines – mathematical, historical, scientific, legal, psychoanalytic, etc. It is the function of a philosophy of language to recognize the specific nature of these disciplines and thereby assign each 'language-game' its due (as Wittgenstein would have it), limiting and correcting their mutual claims. Thus one of the main purposes of hermeneutics is to refer the different uses of language to different regions of being – natural, scientific, fictional, etc. But this is not all. Hermeneutics is also concerned with the permanent spirit of language. By the spirit of language we intend not just some decorative excess or effusion of subjectivity, but *the capacity of language to open up new worlds*. Poetry and myth are not just nostalgia for some forgotten world. They constitute a disclosure of unprecedented worlds, an opening on to other *possible* worlds which transcend the established limits of our *actual* world.

> How then would you situate your philosophy of language in relation to Analytic Philosophy?

I certainly share at least one common concern of Analytic Philosophy: the concern with ordinary language in contradistinction to the scientific language of documentation and verification. Scientific language has no real function of communication or interpersonal dialogue. It is important therefore that we preserve the rights of ordinary language where the communication of experience is of primary significance. But my criticism of ordinary language philosophy is that it does not take into account the fact that language itself is a place of prejudice and bias. Therefore, we need a third dimension of language, a critical and creative dimension, which is directed towards neither scientific verification nor ordinary communication but towards the disclosure of possible worlds. This third dimension of language I call the poetic. The adequate self-understanding of man is dependent on this third dimension of language as a *disclosure of possibility*.

Is not this philosophy of language profoundly phenomenological in character?

Yes it is. Because phenomenology as it emerged in the philosophies of Husserl and Heidegger raised the central question of 'meaning'. And it is here that we find the main dividing line between the structuralist analysis and phenomenological hermeneutics. Whereas the former is concerned with the immanent arrangement of texts and textual codes, hermeneutics looks to the 'meaning' produced by these codes. It is my conviction that the decisive feature of hermeneutics is the capacity of world-disclosure yielded by texts. Hermeneutics is not confined to the *objective* structural analysis of texts nor to the *subjective* existential analysis of the authors of texts; its primary concern is with the *worlds* which these authors and texts open up. It is by an understanding of the worlds, actual and possible, opened by language that we may arrive at a better understanding of ourselves.

Select bibliography of Paul Ricoeur

Gabriel Marcel et Karl Jaspers: Philosophie du mystère et philosophie du paradoxe, Temps présent, Paris, 1947.

Karl Jaspers et la philosophie de l'existence, en collaboration avec M. Dufrenne, Le Seuil, Paris, 1947.

Le Volontaire et l'involontaire, Aubier, Paris, 1950; English translation, *Freedom and Nature: the Voluntary and the Involuntary*, transl. Erazim V. Kohák, Northwestern University Press, Evanston, 1966.

Idées directrices pour une phénoménologie d'Edmund Husserl, traduction et présentation, Gallimard, Paris, 1950; English translation of the introduction to this work is published as Part Two of *Husserl: an Analysis of his Phenomenology*, Northwestern University Press, Evanston, 1967.

Histoire et vérité, Le Seuil, Paris, 1955; English translation, *History and Truth*, transl. Charles A. Kelbley, Northwestern University Press, Evanston, 1965.

Dialogues with contemporary Continental thinkers

L'Homme faillible, Aubier, Paris, 1960; English translation, *Fallible Man*, transl. Charles A. Kelbley, Henry Regnery, Chicago, 1965.

La Symbolique du mal, Aubier, Paris, 1960; English translation, *The Symbolism of Evil*, transl. Emerson Buchanan, Harper & Row, New York, 1967.

De l'interprétation, essai sur Freud, Le Seuil, Paris, 1965; English translation, *Freud and Philosophy: an Essay on Interpretation*, transl. Denis Savage, Yale University Press, New Haven, 1970.

Le Conflit des interprétations, essais d'herméneutique, Le Seuil, Paris, 1969; English translation, *The Conflict of Interpretations: Essays in Hermeneutics*, ed. Don Ihde, transl. Willis Domingo *et al.*, Northwestern University Press, Evanston, 1974.

Political and Social Essays, ed. David Stewart and Joseph Bien, transl. Donald Siewert *et al.*, Ohio University Press, Athens, Ohio, 1974.

La Métaphore vive, Le Seuil, Paris, 1975; English translation, *The Rule of Metaphor: Multi-disciplinary Studies of the Creation of Meaning in Language*, transl. Robert Czerny, Routledge and Kegan Paul, London, 1978.

Interpretation Theory: Discourse and the Surplus of Meaning, Texas Christian University Press, Fort Worth, 1976.

The Philosophy of Paul Ricoeur: an Anthology of His Work, ed. Charles E. Reagan and David Stewart, Beacon Press, Boston, 1978.

Hermeneutics and the Human Sciences, ed. and transl. John B. Thompson, Cambridge University Press and Editions de la Maison des Sciences de l'Homme, 1981.

Temps et récit, Le Seuil, Paris, 1983.

Emmanuel Lévinas

Prefatory note

Emmanuel Lévinas was born in Kaunas, Lithuania in 1906 to a Jewish family. He later moved to the Ukraine, where he lived through the Russian Revolution in 1917, before finally departing as a young man for France, where he spent most of his adult life. In 1923, Lévinas began to study philosophy at Strasbourg University, where he was taught by Blondel, Pradines and later by Héring, who first introduced him to phenomenology in 1927. During these student years, Lévinas also made the acquaintance of Maurice Blanchot and was deeply impressed by both the repercussions of the Dreyfus affair and the emergence of Zionism which he described as 'the vision of a strange startling new advent of a people, on a par with all humanity'.

In 1928 Lévinas travelled to Freiburg University in Germany to pursue his studies of phenomenology with Husserl and Heidegger, whose monumental *Being and Time* had just been published. This brief apprenticeship with the 'masters' (Lévinas returned to France in 1929) was to prove a lifelong inspiration for Lévinas. His first three major publications – *La Théorie de l'intuition dans la phénoménologie de Husserl* (1930), *De l'existence à l'existant* (1947) and *En découvrant l'existence avec Husserl et Heidegger* (1949) – were written from an explicitly phenomenological standpoint.

Lévinas became a French citizen in 1930 and began to frequent the avant-garde philosophical groups of Gabriel Marcel and Jean Wahl in Paris. Indeed it was during the thirties and forties that he became familiar with the more 'existentialist' brand of phenomenology practised in France. Although he has lectured frequently in Israel and Belgium, Lévinas has worked and taught in France for most of his life, serving as Director of *l'Ecole Normale Israélite Orientale* and as Professor of Philosophy at the universities of Poitiers, Paris–Nanterre and the Sorbonne.

Lévinas' most influential work is undoubtedly *Totality and Infinity*, first published in 1961. Here Lévinas deploys the phenomenological method to describe two basic kinds of relationship to the world: (1) an 'ontological' relationship which centralizes our experience in terms of Being-as-a-totality (be it the Being of our subjective *cogito* or the Being of the immanent, finite *cosmos*); and (2) a 'metaphysical' relationship which decentralizes our experience and opens us to the infinite otherness of transcendence. While the former favours a *philosophy of nature*, whereby the human subject can be accorded its place in the totalizing scheme of things, the latter endorses the primacy of an *ethical philosophy* which shows how man's relationship to man can transcend the natural rapport of possession, power and belongingness, in search of a Good beyond Being. Lévinas argues that the mainstream of Western philosophy represents a totalizing ontology, running from the pre-Socratics up to Hegel and Heidegger, which seeks to reduce 'difference' and 'otherness' to the category of the 'same'. Over against this ontological tradition, he champions the alternative and usually ignored counter-tradition of 'metaphysics' to which, he claims, Plato's notion of the Good, and Descartes 'Idea of the Infinite' belong in so far as they surpass the totalizing categories of Being. In short, Lévinas' phenomenological descriptions of our finite being-in-the-world (*être-au-monde*) lead him ultimately beyond the limits of phenomenology to an ethics of transcendence based on the primacy of the *other* over the *same*.

While Lévinas remains cautious in his early work about identifying the relationship with the other as religious, from the sixties onwards he wrote a number of studies on Judaism – including *Difficile liberté* (1963), *Quatre lectures talmudiques* (1968) and *Du sacré au Saint* (1977) – in which he argues that the Hebraic tradition differs from its Hellenic counterpart in affirming that God as the absolutely Other can only be encountered in and through our ethical rapport with our fellow humans (what he terms the 'face to face relationship'). The biblical and Talmudic texts, he claims, teach us that the 'I' does not begin with itself in some pure moment of autonomous self-consciousness but in relation with the other, for whom it remains forever responsible. The overall purpose of

Lévinas' thought is, accordingly, to turn knowledge into 'an act of unsettling its own natural condition' as power and violence in order to open it to the infinity of the other who transcends every attempt to reduce him to our totalizing grasp. 'To exist', writes Lévinas, 'has a meaning in another dimension than that of the perduration of the totality; it can go beyond Being'.

The dialogue that follows took place in Paris in 1981.

Ethics of the infinite

> **Richard Kearney:** Perhaps you could retrace your philosophical itinerary by identifying some of the major influences on your thought?

Emmanuel Lévinas: Apart from the great masters of the history of philosophy – in particular Plato, Descartes and Kant – the first contemporary influence on my own thinking was Bergson. In 1925, in Strasbourg University, Bergson was being hailed as France's leading thinker. For example, Blondel, one of his Strasbourg disciples, developed a specifically Bergsonian psychology quite hostile to Freud – a hostility which made a deep and lasting impression on me. Moreover, Bergson's theory of time as concrete duration (*la durée concrète*) is, I believe, one of the most significant, if largely ignored, contributions to contemporary philosophy. Indeed, it was this Bergsonian emphasis on temporality that prepared the soil for the subsequent implantation of Heideggerian phenomenology into France. It is all the more ironic, therefore, that in *Being and Time* Heidegger unjustly accuses Bergson of reducing time to space. What is more, in Bergson's *L'Evolution créatrice*, one finds the whole notion of technology as the destiny of the Western philosophy of Reason. Bergson was the first to contrast technology, as a logical and necessary expression of scientific rationality, with an alternative form of human expression which he called creative intuition or impulse – the *élan vital*. All of Heidegger's celebrated analyses of our technological era as the logical culmination of Western metaphysics and its forgetfulness of Being came after Bergson's reflections on the subject. Bergson's importance to contemporary Continental thought has been somewhat obfuscated; he has been suspended in a sort of limbo; but I believe it is only a temporary suspension.

> Could you describe how, after Bergson, you came under the influence of the German phenomenologists, Husserl and Heidegger?

It was in 1927 that I first became interested in Husserl's phenomenology which was still unknown in France at that time. I travelled to the University of Freiburg for two semesters in 1928–9 and studied phenomenology with Husserl and also, of course, with Heidegger, who was then the leading light in German philosophy after the publication of *Sein und Zeit* in 1927. Phenomenology represented the second, but undoubtedly most important, philosophical influence on my thinking. Indeed, from the point of view of philosophical method and discipline, I remain to this day a phenomenologist.

> How would you characterize the particular contribution of phenomenology to modern philosophy?

The most fundamental contribution of Husserl's phenomenology is its methodical disclosure of how meaning comes to be, how it emerges in our consciousness of the world, or more precisely, in our becoming conscious of our intentional rapport (*visée*) with the world. The phenomenological method enables us to discover meaning within our lived experience; it reveals consciousness to be an intentionality always in *contact* with objects outside of itself, other than itself. Human experience is not some self-transparent substance or pure *cogito*; it is always intending or tending towards something in the world which preoccupies it. The phenomenological method permits consciousness to understand its own preoccupations, to reflect upon itself and thus discover all the hidden or neglected horizons of its intentionality. In other words, by returning to the implicit horizons of consciousness, phenomenology enables us to explicate or unfold the full intentional meaning of an object, which would otherwise be presented as an abstract and isolated entity cut off from its intentional horizons. Phenomenology thus teaches us that consciousness is at once tied to the object of its experience and yet free to detach itself from this object in order to return upon itself, focusing on those *visées* of intentionality in which the object emerges as *meaningful*, as part of our lived experience. One might say that phenomenology is a way of becoming aware of where we are in the world, a *sich besinnen* which consists of a recovery of the origin of meaning in our lifeworld or *Lebenswelt*.

Your second major work was entitled *En découvrant l'existence avec Husserl et Heidegger*. If Husserl introduced you to the phenomenological method, how would you assess your debt to Heidegger?

Heidegger's philosophy was a shock for me, and for most of my contempories in the late twenties and thirties. It completely altered the course and character of European philosophy. I think that one cannot seriously philosophize today without traversing the Heideggerian path in some form or other. *Being and Time*, which is much more significant and profound than any of Heidegger's later works, represents the fruition and flowering of Husserlian phenomenology. The most far-reaching potentialities of the phenomenological method were exploited by Heidegger in this early work and particularly in his phenomenological analysis of 'anguish' as the fundamental mood of our existence. Heidegger brilliantly described how this existential mood or *Stimmung* revealed the way in which we were attuned to Being. Human moods, such as guilt, fear, anxiety, joy or dread, are no longer considered as mere physiological sensations or psychological emotions, but are now recognized as the ontological ways in which we feel and find our being-in-the-world, our being-there as *Befindlichkeit*.

This phenomenological analysis of our existential moods was, of course, something which you yourself used to original effect in your descriptions of such human dispositions as need, desire, effort, laziness and insomnia in *De l'existence à l'existant*. But to return to Husserl and Heidegger, how would you define the main difference of *style* in their employment of phenomenology?

Husserl's approach was always more abstract and ponderous – one really had to have one's ears cocked if one wished to understand his lectures! Husserl was primarily concerned with establishing and perfecting phenomenology as a method, that is, as an epistemological method of describing how our logical concepts and categories emerge and assume an essential meaning. What is the relation between our logical judgements and our perceptual experience? This was Husserl's question – and phenomenology was his method of responding by means of rigorous and exact descriptions of our intentional modes of consciousness. Phenomenology was thus a way of suspending our preconceptions and prejudices in order to disclose how essential truth and meaning are generated; it was a methodical return to the beginnings, to the origins of knowledge. On the other hand, Heidegger, the young disciple, brought the phenomenological method to life and gave it a contemporary style and relevance. Heidegger's existential analyses possessed a poetic quality and force which enchanted and astonished the mind, while preserving all the while the rigorous contours of the master's method. So that I would say, by way of summary, that if it was Husserl who opened up for me the radical possibilities of a phenomenological analysis of knowledge, it was Heidegger who first gave these possibilities a positive and concrete grounding in our everyday existence; Heidegger showed that the phenomenological search for eternal truths and essences ultimately originates in *time*, in our temporal and historical existence.

> Your first study of phenomenology, *La Théorie de l'intuition dans la phénoménologie de Husserl*, published in 1930, was the first complete work on Husserl in French. Your seminal study of Heidegger in *La Revue philosophique* in 1931 was another milestone in contemporary French philosophy. Sartre and Merleau-Ponty were soon to follow suit, exploring further possibilities of the phenomenological method known today as French existentialism. As the discreet inaugurator of the French interest in phenomenology, what exactly was your relationship with Sartre and Merleau-Ponty?

I have always admired the powerful originality of Merleau-Ponty's work, however different from my own in many respects, and had frequent contact with him at Jean Wahl's philosophical meetings in the *Collège de Philosophie* in the thirties and forties, and also whenever I contributed to *Les Temps modernes* while he was still co-editor with Sartre. But it was Sartre who guaranteed my place in eternity by stating in his famous obituary essay on Merleau-Ponty that he, Sartre, 'was introduced to phenomenology by Lévinas'. Simone de Beauvoir tells how it happened in one of her autobiographical works. One day in the early thirties Sartre chanced upon a copy of my book on Husserl in the Picard bookshop just opposite the Sorbonne. He picked it up, read it and declared to de Beauvoir, 'This is the philosophy I wanted to write!' Afterwards he reassured himself that my analysis was far too didactic and that he could do better himself! And so he applied himself to a sustained study of Husserl and Heidegger. The result was a host of enterprising phenomenological analyses ranging from *L'Imaginaire* (1935) to *L'Etre et le néant* (1945). I was extremely interested in Sartre's phenomenological analysis of the 'other', though I always regretted that he interpreted it as a threat and a degradation, an interpretation which also found expression in his fear of the God question. In fact, Sartre's rejection of theism was so unequivocal that his final statements, in the *Nouvel Observateur* interviews just before his death, about the legitimacy of Jewish history as a belief in the existence of God seemed incredible to those who knew him or had studied him. In Sartre the phenomenon of the other was still considered, as in all Western ontology, to be a modality of unity and fusion, that is a reduction of the other to the categories of the same. This is described by Sartre as a teleological project to unite and totalize the for-itself and the in-itself, the self and the other-than-self. It is here that my fundamental philosophical disagreement with Sartre lay. At a personal level, I always liked Sartre. I first met him in Gabriel Marcel's house just before the war and had further dealings with him after the war on the controversial question of Israel's existence. Sartre had refused the Nobel Prize for Literature and I felt that someone who had the courage to reject such a prize for ethical reasons had certainly conserved the right to intervene and to try to persuade Nasser, the Egyptian leader at the time, to forego his threats to Israel and embark upon dialogue. What I also admired in Sartre was that his philosophy was not confined to purely conceptual issues but was open to the possibility of ethical and political commitment.

What are the origins of the religious dimensions in your own thinking?

I was born in Lithuania, a country where Jewish culture was intellectually prized and fostered and where the interpretation and exegesis of biblical texts was cultivated to a high degree. It was here that I first learned to read the Bible in Hebrew. It was at a much later date, however, that I became actively interested in Jewish thought. After the Second World War I encountered a remarkable master of Talmudic interpretation here in Paris, a man of exceptional mental agility who taught me how to read the Rabbinic texts. He taught me for four years, from 1947 to 1951, and what I myself have written in my *Talmudic Lectures* has been written in the shadow of his shadow. It was this post-war encounter which reactivated my latent – I might even say dormant – interest in the Judaic tradition. But when I acknowledge this Judaic influence, I do not wish to talk in terms of belief or non-belief. 'Believe' is not a verb to be employed in the first person singular. Nobody can really say *I believe* – or *I do not believe* for that matter – that God exists. The existence of God is not a question of an individual soul uttering logical syllogisms. It cannot be proved. The existence of God, the *SeinGottes*, is sacred history itself, the sacredness of man's relation to man through which God may pass. God's existence is the story of his revelation in biblical history.

How do you reconcile the phenomenological and religious dimensions of your thinking?

I always make a clear distinction, in what I write, between philosophical and confessional texts. I do not deny that they may ultimately have a common source of inspiration. I simply state that it is necessary to draw a line of demarcation between them as distinct methods of exegesis, as separate languages. I would never, for example, introduce a Talmudic or biblical verse into one of my philosophical texts to try to prove or justify a phenomenological argument.

Would you go so far as to endorse Heidegger's argument that genuine philosophical questioning requires one to suspend or bracket one's religious faith? I am thinking in particular of Heidegger's statement in his *Introduction to Metaphysics* that a religious thinker cannot ask the philosophical question, 'Why is there something rather than nothing?' – since he already possesses the answer: 'Because God created the world.' Hence Heidegger's conclusion that a religious (in the sense of Christian or Jewish) philosophy is a square circle, a contradiction in terms.

For me the essential characteristic of philosophy is a certain, specifically Greek, way of thinking and speaking. Philosophy is primarily a question of language; and it is by identifying the subtextual language of particular discourses that we can decide whether they are philosophical or not. Philosophy employs a series of terms and concepts – such as *morphe* (form), *ousia* (substance), *nous* (reason), *logos* (thought) or *telos* (goal), etc. – which constitute a specifically Greek lexicon of intelligibility. French and German, and indeed all of Western philosophy is entirely shot through with this specific language; it is a token of the genius of Greece to have been able to thus deposit its language in the basket of Europe. But although philosophy is essentially Greek, it is not exclusively so. It also has sources and roots which are non-Greek. What we term the Judeo-Christian tradition, for example, proposed an alternative approach to meaning and truth. The difficulty is, of course, to *speak* of this alternative tradition given the essentially Greek nature of philosophical language. And this difficulty is compounded by the fact that Judeo-Christian culture has, historically, been incorporated into Greek philosophy. It is virtually impossible for philosophers today to have recourse to an unalloyed religious language. All one can say is that the Septennium is not yet complete, that the translation of biblical wisdom into the Greek language remains unfinished. The best one can do by way of identifying the fundamental difference between the Greek and biblical approaches to truth is to try to define the distinctive quality of Greek philosophy before the historical incursion of Jewish and Christian cultures. Perhaps the most essential distinguishing feature of the language of Greek philosophy was its equation of truth with an *intelligibility of presence*. By this I mean an intelligibility which considers truth to be that which is present or co-present, that which can be gathered or synchronized into a totality which we would call the world or *cosmos*. According to the Greek model, intelligibility is what can be rendered present, what can be represented in some eternal here-and-now, exposed and disclosed in pure light. To thus equate truth with presence is to presume that however different the two terms of a relation might appear (e.g. the Divine and the human) or however separated over time (e.g. into past and future), they can ultimately be rendered commensurate and simultaneous, the same, englobed in a history which totalizes time into a beginning or an end, or both, which is presence. The Greek notion of Being is essentially this presence.

Would you agree then with Heidegger's critique of Western metaphysics as a philosophy of presence?

I don't think Heidegger is entirely consistent on this point. For me, Heidegger never really escaped from the Greek language of intelligibility and presence. Even though he spent much of his philosophical career struggling against certain metaphysical notions of presence – in particular the objectifying notion of presence as *Vorhandenheit* which expresses itself in our scientific and technological categorization of the world – he ultimately seems to espouse another, more subtle and complex, notion of presence as *Anwesen*, that is, the coming-into-presence of Being. Thus, while Heidegger heralds the end of the metaphysics of presence, he continues to think of Being as a coming-into-presence; he seems unable to break away from the hegemony of presence which he denounces. This ambiguity also comes to the surface when Heidegger interprets our being-in-the-world as history. The ultimate and most authentic mission of existence or *Dasein* is to recollect (*wiederholen*) and totalize its temporal dispersal into past, present and future. *Dasein* is its history to the extent that it can interpret and narrate its existence as a finite and contemporaneous story (*histoire*), a totalizing co-presence of past, present and future.

How does the ethical relation to the other, so central a theme in your philosophy, serve to subvert the ontology of presence in its Greek and Heideggerian forms?

The interhuman relationship emerges with our history, with our being-in-the-world as intelligibility and presence. The interhuman realm can thus be construed as a part of the disclosure of the world as presence. But it can also be considered from another perspective – the ethical or biblical perspective which transcends the Greek language of intelligibility – as a theme of justice and concern for the other as other, as a theme of love and desire which carries us beyond the finite Being of the world as presence. The interhuman is thus an interface: a double axis where what is 'of the world' qua *phenomenological intelligibility* is juxtaposed with what is 'not of the world' qua *ethical responsibility*. It is in this ethical perspective that God must be thought and not in the ontological perspective of our being-there or of some Supreme Being and Creator correlative to the world, as traditional metaphysics often held. God, as the God of alterity and transcendence, can only be understood in terms of that interhuman dimension which, to be sure, emerges in the phenomenological–ontological perspective of the intelligible world, but which cuts through and perforates the totality of presence and points towards the absolutely Other. In this sense one could say that biblical thought has, to some extent, influenced my ethical reading of the interhuman, whereas Greek thought has largely determined its philosophical expression in language. So that I would maintain, against Heidegger, that philosophy can be ethical as well as ontological, can be at once Greek and non-Greek in its inspiration. These two sources of inspiration coexist as two different tendencies in modern philosophy and it is my own personal task to try to identify this dual origin of meaning – *der Ursprung der Sinnhaften* – in the interhuman relationship.

> One of the most complex and indeed central themes in your philosophy is the rapport between the interhuman and time. Could you elucidate this rapport by situating it in terms of the ethics/ontology distinction?

I am trying to show that man's ethical relation to the other is ultimately prior to his ontological relation to himself (egology) or to the totality of things which we call the world (cosmology). The relationship with the other is *time*: it is an untotalizable diachrony in which one moment pursues another without ever being able to retrieve it, to catch up with or coincide with it. The non-simultaneous and non-present is my primary rapport with the other in time. Time means that the other is forever beyond me, irreducible to the synchrony of the same. The temporality of the interhuman opens up the meaning of otherness and the otherness of meaning. But because there are more than two people in the world, we invariably pass from the ethical perspective of alterity to the ontological perspective of totality. There are always at least three persons. This means that we are obliged to ask who is the other, to try to objectively define the undefinable, to compare the incomparable in an effort to juridically hold different positions together. So that the first type of simultaneity is the simultaneity of equality, the attempt to reconcile and balance the conflicting claims of each person. If there were only two people in the world, there would be no need for law courts because I would always be responsible for, and before, the other. As soon as there are three, the ethical relationship with the other becomes political and enters into the totalizing discourse of ontology. We can never completely escape from the language of ontology and politics. Even when we deconstruct ontology we are obliged to use its language. Derrida's work of deconstruction, for example, possesses the speculative and methodological rigour of the philosophy which he is seeking to deconstruct. It's like the argument of the sceptics: how can we know that we can't know anything? The greatest virtue of philosophy is that it can put itself in question, try to deconstruct what it has constructed and unsay what it has said. Science, on the contrary, does not try to unsay itself, does not interrogate or challenge its own concepts, terms or foundations; it forges ahead, progresses. In this respect, science attempts to ignore language by constructing its own abstract non-language of calculable symbols and formulae. But science is merely a secondary bracketing of philosophical language from which it is ultimately derived; it can never have the last word. Heidegger summed this up admirably when he declared that science *calculates* but does not *think*. Now what I am interested in is precisely this ability of philosophy to think, to question itself and ultimately to unsay itself. And I wonder if this capacity for interrogation and for unsaying (*dédire*) is not itself derived from the pre-ontological interhuman relationship with the other. The fact that philosophy cannot fully totalize the alterity of meaning in some final presence or simultaneity is not for me a deficiency or fault. Or to put it in another way, the best thing about philosophy is that it fails. It is better that philosophy fail to totalize meaning – even though, as ontology, it has attempted just this – for it thereby remains open to the irreducible otherness of transcendence. Greek ontology, to be sure, expressed the strong sentiment that the last word is unity, the many becoming one, the truth as synthesis. Hence Plato defined love – *eros* – as only *half*-divine in so far as it lacks the full coincidence or unification of differences which he defined as divinity. The whole Romantic tradition in European poetry tends to conform to this Platonic ontology by inferring that love is perfect when two people become *one*. I am trying to work against this identification of the Divine with unification or totality. Man's relationship with the other is *better* as difference than as unity: sociality is better than fusion. The very value of love is the impossibility of reducing the other to myself, of coinciding into sameness. From an ethical perspective, two have a better time than one (*on s'amuse mieux à deux*)!

Is it possible to conceive of an eschatology of non-coincidence wherein man and God could coexist eternally without fusing into oneness?

But why eschatology? Why should we wish to reduce time to eternity? Time is the most profound relationship that man can have with God precisely as a going towards God. There is an excellence in time which would be lost in eternity. To desire eternity is to desire to perpetuate oneself, to go on living as oneself, to *be* always. Can one conceive of an eternal life that would not suspend time or reduce it to a contemporaneous presence? To accept time is to accept death as the impossibility of presence. To be in eternity is to be *one*, to be *oneself* eternally. To be in time is to be for God (*être à Dieu*), a perpetual leavetaking (*adieu*).

But how can one be for God or go towards God as the absolutely Other? Is it by going towards the human other?

Yes, and it is essential to point out that the relation implied in the preposition *towards* (*à*) is ultimately a relation derived from time. Time fashions man's relation to the other, and to the absolutely Other or God, as a diachronic relation irreducible to correlation. 'Going towards God' is not to be understood here in the classical ontological sense of a return to, or reunification with, God as the Beginning or End of temporal existence. 'Going towards God' is meaningless unless seen in terms of my primary going towards the other person. I can only go towards God by being ethically concerned by and for the other person. I am not saying that ethics presupposes belief. On the contrary, belief presupposes ethics as that disruption of our being-in-the-world which opens us to the other. The ethical exigency to be responsible for the other undermines the ontological primacy of the meaning of Being; it unsettles the natural and political positions we have taken up in the world and predisposes us to a meaning that is other than Being, that is otherwise than Being (*autrement qu'être*).

What role does your analysis of the 'face' (*visage*) of the other play in this disruption of ontology?

The approach to the face is the most basic mode of responsibility. As such, the face of the other is verticality and uprightness; it spells a relation of rectitude. The face is not in front of me (*en face de moi*) but above me; it is the other before death, looking through and exposing death. Secondly, the face is the other who asks me not to let him die alone, as if to do so were to become an accomplice in his death. Thus the face says to me: you shall not kill. In the relation to the face I am exposed as a usurper of the place of the other. The celebrated 'right to existence' which Spinoza called the *conatus essendi* and defined as the basic principle of all intelligibility, is challenged by the relation to the face. Accordingly, my duty to respond to the other suspends my natural right to self-survival, *le droit vitale*. My ethical relation of love for the other stems from the fact that the self cannot survive by itself alone, cannot find meaning within its own being-in-the-world, within the ontology of sameness. That is why I prefaced *Totality and Infinity* with Pascal's phrase, '*Ma place au soleil, le commencement de toute usurpation*'. Pascal makes the same point when he declares that '*le moi est haïssable*'. Pascal's ethical sentiments here go against the ontological privileging of 'the right to exist'. To expose myself to the vulnerability of the face is to put my ontological right to existence into question. In ethics, the other's right to exist has primacy over my own, a primacy epitomized in the ethical edict: you shall not kill, you shall not jeopardize the life of the other. The ethical rapport with the face is asymmetrical in that it subordinates my existence to the other. This principle recurs in Darwinian biology as the 'survival of the fittest', and in psychoanalysis as the natural instinct of the 'id' for gratification, possession and power – the *libido dominandi*.

So I owe more to the other than to myself . . .

Absolutely, and this ethical exigency undermines the Hellenic endorsement, still prevalent today, of the *conatus essendi*. There is a Jewish proverb which says that 'the other's material needs are my spritual needs'; it is this disproportion or asymmetry which characterizes the ethical refusal of the first truth of ontology – the struggle to *be*. Ethics is, therefore, *against nature* because it forbids the murderousness of my natural will to put my own existence first.

Does going towards God always require that we go against nature?

God cannot appear as the cause or creator of nature. The word of God speaks through the glory of the face and calls for an ethical conversion or reversal of our nature. What we call lay morality, that is, humanistic concern for our fellow human beings, already speaks the voice of God. But the moral priority of the other over myself could not come to be if it were not motivated by something beyond nature. The ethical situation is a human situation, beyond human nature, in which the idea of God comes to mind (*Gott fällt mir ein*). In this respect, we could say that God is the other who turns our nature inside out, who calls our ontological will-to-be into question. This ethical call of conscience occurs, no doubt, in other religious systems besides the Judeo-Christian, but it remains an essentially religious vocation. God does indeed go against nature for He is not of this world. God is other than Being.

How does one distil the ethico-religious meaning of existence from its natural or ontological sedimentation?

But your question already assumes that ethics is derived from ontology. I believe, on the contrary, that the ethical relationship with the other is just as primary and original (*ursprünglich*) as ontology – if not more so. Ethics is not derived from an ontology of nature; it is its opposite, a meontology which affirms a meaning beyond Being, a primary mode of non-Being (*me-on*).

And yet you claim that the ethical and the ontological coexist as two inspirations without Western philosophy?

Already in Greek philosophy one can discern traces of the ethical breaking through the ontological, for example in Plato's idea of the 'Good existing beyond Being' (*agathon epekeina tes ousias*). (Heidegger, of course, contests this ethical reading of the Good in Plato, maintaining that it is merely one among other descriptions of Being itself.) One can also cite in this connection Descartes' discovery of the 'Idea of the Infinite', which surpasses the finite limits of human nature and the human mind. And similarly supra-ontological notions are to be found in the pseudo-Dionysian doctrine of the *via eminentiae* with its surplus of the Divine over Being, or in the Augustinian distinction in the *Confessions* between the truth which challenges (*veritas redarguens*) and the ontological truth which shines (*veritas lucens*), etc.

Do you think that Husserl's theory of temporality points to an otherness beyond Being?

However radically Husserl's theory of time may gesture in this direction, particularly in *The Phenomenology of Internal Time*

Consciousness, it remains overall a *cosmological* notion of time; temporality continues to be thought of in terms of the present, in terms of an ontology of presence. The present (*Gegenwart*) remains for Husserl the centralizing dimension of time, the past and the future being defined in terms of intentional re-presentations (*Vergegenwärtigen*). To be more precise, the past, Husserl claims, is retained by the present and the future is pre-contained in, or protended by, the present. Time past and time future are merely modifications of the present; and this double extension of the present into the past (retention) and the future (protension) reinforces the ontology of presence as a seizure and appropriation of what is other or transcendent. Heidegger, who actually edited Husserl's lectures on time, introduced an element of alterity into his own phenomenological description of time in *Being and Time*, when he analysed time in terms of our anguish before death. Temporality is now disclosed as an ecstatic being-towards-death which releases us from the present into an ultimate horizon of possibles, rather than as a holdng or seizing or retaining of the present.

> But is not Heidegger's analysis of temporality as a being-towards-death still a subtle form of extending what is *mine*, of reducing the world to *my* ownmost (*eigenst*) authentic (*eigentlich*) existence? Death is for Heidegger always *my* death. *Dasein* is always the Being which is *mine*.

This is the fundamental difference between my ethical analysis of death and Heidegger's ontological analysis. Whereas for Heidegger death is *my* death, for me it is the *other*'s death. In *The Letter on Humanism*, Heidegger defines *Dasein* in almost Darwinian fashion as 'a being which is concerned for its own being'. In paragraph 9 of *Being and Time*, he defines the main characteristic of *Dasein* as that of *mineness* (*Jemeinigkeit*), the way in which Being becomes mine, imposes or imprints itself on me. *Jemeinigkeit* as the possession of my Being as *mine* precedes the articulation of the *I*. *Dasein* is only 'I' (*Ich*) because it is already *Jemeinigkeit*. I become I only because I possess my own Being as primary. For ethical thought, on the contrary, *le moi*, as this primacy of what is mine, is *haïssable*. Ethics is not, for this reason, a depersonalizing exigency. I am defined as a subjectivity, as a singular person, as an 'I', precisely because I am exposed to the other. It is my inescapable and incontrovertible answerability to the other that makes me an individual 'I'. So that I become a responsible or ethical 'I' to the extent that I agree to depose or dethrone myself – to abdicate my position of centrality – in favour of the vulnerable other. As the Bible says: 'He who loses his soul gains it'. The ethical I is a being who asks if he has a right to be!, who excuses himself to the other for his own existence.

> In the structuralist and post-structuralist debates which have tended to dominate Continental philosophy in recent years, there has been much talk of the disappearance or the demise of the subject. Is your ethical thought an attempt to preserve subjectivity in some form?

My thinking on this matter goes in the opposite direction to structuralism. It is not that I wish to preserve, over and against the structuralist critique, the idea of a subject who would be a substantial or mastering centre of meaning, an idealist self-sufficient *cogito*. These traditional ontological versions of subjectivity have nothing to do with the meontological version of subjectivity that I put forward in *Autrement qu'être*. Ethical subjectivity dispenses with the idealizing subjectivity of ontology which reduces everything to itself. The ethical 'I' is subjectivity precisely in so far as it kneels before the other, sacrificing its own liberty to the more primordial call of the other. For me, the freedom of the subject is not the highest or primary value. The heteronomy of our response to the human other, or to God as the absolutely Other, precedes the autonomy of our subjective freedom. As soon as I acknowledge that it is 'I' who am responsible, I accept that my freedom is anteceded by an obligation to the other. Ethics redefines subjectivity as this heteronymous responsibility in contrast to autonomous freedom. Even if I deny my primordial responsibility to the other by affirming my own freedom as primary, I can never escape the fact that the other has demanded a response from me *before* I affirm my freedom not to respond to his demand. Ethical freedom is *une difficile liberté*, a heteronymous freedom obliged to the other. Consequently, the other is the richest and the poorest of beings: the richest, at an ethical level, in that it always comes before me, its right-to-be preceding mine; the poorest, at an ontological or political level, in that without me it can do nothing, it is utterly vulnerable and exposed. The other haunts our ontological existence and keeps the psyche awake, in a state of vigilant insomnia. Even though we are ontologically free to refuse the other, we remain forever accused, with a bad conscience.

> Is not the ethical obligation to the other a purely negative ideal, impossible to realize in our everyday being-in-the-world? After all, we live in a concrete historical world governed by ontological drives and practices, be they political and institutional totalities or technological systems of mastery, organization and control. Is ethics practicable in human society as we know it? Or is it merely an invitation to apolitical acquiescence?

This is a fundamental point. Of course we inhabit an ontological world of technological mastery and political self-preservation. Indeed without these political and technological structures of organization we would not be able to feed mankind. This is the great paradox of human existence: we must use the ontological *for the sake of the other*; to ensure the survival of the other we must resort to the technico-political systems of means and ends. This same paradox is also present in our use of language, to return to an earlie point. We have no option but to employ the language and concepts of Greek philosophy even in our attempts to go beyond them. We cannot obviate the language of metaphysics and yet we cannot, ethically speaking, be satisfied with it: it is necessary but not enough. I disagree, however, with Derrida's interpretation of this paradox. Whereas he tends to see the deconstruction of the Western metaphysics of presence as an irredeemable crisis, I see it as a golden opportunity for Western philosophy to open itself to the dimension of otherness and transcendence beyond Being.

> Is there any sense in which language can be ethical?

In *Autrement qu'être* I pose this question when I ask: 'What is saying without a said?'. Saying is ethical sincerity in so far as it is exposition. As such this *saying* is irreducible to the ontological definability of the *said*. Saying is what makes the self-exposure of sincerity possible; it is a way of giving everything, of not keeping anything for oneself. In so far as ontology equates truth with the intelligibility of total presence, it reduces the pure exposure of saying to the totalizing closure of the said. The child is a pure exposure of expression in so far as it is pure vulnerability; it has not yet learned to dissemble, to deceive, to be insincere. What distinguishes human language from animal or child expression, for example, is that the human speaker can remain silent, can refuse to be exposed in sincerity. The human being is characterized as human not only because he is a being who can speak but also because he is a being who can lie, who can live in the duplicity of language as the dual possibility of exposure and deception. The animal is incapable of this duplicity; the dog, for instance, cannot suppress its bark, the bird its song. But man can repress his saying, and this ability to keep silent, to withold oneself, is the ability to be political. Man can give himself in saying to the point of poetry – or he can withdraw into the non-saying of lies. Language as *saying* is an ethical openness to the other; as that which is *said* – reduced to a fixed identity or synchronized presence – it is an ontological closure to the other.

> But is there not some sort of 'morality' of the *said* which might reflect the ethics of *saying* in our everyday transactions in society? In other words, if politics cannot be ethical in so far as it is an expression of our ontological nature, can it at least be 'moral' (in your sense of that term)?

This distinction between the ethical and the moral is very important here. By morality I mean a series of rules relating to social behaviour and civic duty. But while morality thus operates in the socio-political order of organizing and improving our human survival, it is ultimately founded on an ethical responsibility towards the other. As *prima philosophia*, ethics cannot itself legislate for society or produce rules of conduct whereby society might be revolutionized or transformed. It does not operate at the level of the manifesto or *rappel à l'ordre*; it is not a *savoir vivre*. When I talk of ethics as a 'disinterestedness' (*dès-intér-essement*), I do not mean that it is indifference; I simply mean that it is a form of vigilant passivity to the call of the other which precedes our interest in Being, our *inter-esse* as a being-in-the-world attached to property and appropriating what is other than itself to itself. Morality is what governs the world of political 'interestedness', the social interchanges between citizens in a society. Ethics, as the extreme exposure and sensitivity of one subjectivity to another, becomes morality and hardens its skin as soon as we move into the political world of the impersonal 'third' – the world of government, institutions, tribunals, prisons, schools, committees, etc. But the norm which must continue to inspire and direct the moral order is the ethical norm of the interhuman. If the moral–political order totally relinquishes its ethical foundation, it must accept all forms of society including the fascist or totalitarian, for it can no longer evaluate or discriminate between them. The state is usually better than anarchy – but not always. In some instances, fascism or totalitarianism, for example, the political order of the state may have to be challenged in the name of our ethical responsibility to the other. This is why ethical philosophy must remain the first philosophy.

> Is not the ethical criterion of the interhuman employed by you as a sort of messianic eschatology wherein the ontological structures of possession and totality would be transcended towards a face-to-face relation of pure exposure to the absolutely Other?

Here again I must express my reservations about the term eschatology. The term *eschaton* implies that there might exist a finality, an end (*fin*) to the historical relation of difference between man and the absolutely Other, a reduction of the gap which safeguards the alterity of the transcendent, to a totality of sameness. To realize the *eschaton* would therefore mean that we could seize or appropriate God as a *telos* and degrade the infinite relation with the other to a finite fusion. This is what Hegelian dialectics amounts to, a radical denial of the rupture between the ontological and the ethical. The danger of eschatology is the temptation to consider the man–God relation as a state, as a fixed and permanent state of affairs. I have described ethical responsibility as *insomnia* or *wakefulness* precisely because it is a perpetual duty of vigilance and effort which can never slumber. Ontology as a state of affairs can afford sleep. But love cannot sleep, can never be peaceful or permanent. Love is the incessant watching over of the other; it can never be satisfied or contented with the bourgeois ideal of love as domestic comfort or the mutual possession of two people living out an *egoisme-à-deux*.

> If you reject the term 'eschatology', would you accept the term 'messianic' to describe this ethical relation with the other?

Only if one understands messianic here according to the Talmudic maxim that 'the doctors of the law will never have peace, neither in this world nor in the next; they go from meeting to meeting discussing always – for there is always more to be discussed'. I could not accept a form of messianism which would terminate the need for discussion, which would end our watchfulness.

But are we not ethically obliged to struggle for a perfect world of peace?

Yes, but I seek this peace not for *me* but for the other. By contrast, if I say that 'virtue is its own reward' I can only say so *for myself*; as soon as I make this a standard for the other I exploit him, for what I am then saying is: be virtuous towards me – work for me, love me, serve me, etc. – but don't expect anything from me in return. That would be rather like the story of the Czar's mother who goes to the hospital and says to the dying soldier: 'You must be very happy to die for your country.' I must always demand more of myself than of the other; and this is why I disagree with Buber's description of the I–Thou ethical relation as a symmetrical co-presence. As Alyosha Karamazov says in *The Brothers Karamazov* by Dostoyevsky: 'We are all responsible for everyone else – but I am more responsible than all the others.' And he does not mean that every 'I' is more responsible than all the others, for that would be to generalize the law for everyone else – to demand as much from the other as I do from myself. This essential asymmetry is the very basis of ethics: not only am I more responsible than the other but I am even responsible for everyone else's responsibility!

How does the God of ethics differ from the 'God of the philosophers', that is, the God of traditional ontology?

For ethics, it is only in the infinite relation with the other that God passes (*se passe*), that traces of God are to be found. God thus reveals himself as a trace, not as an ontological presence which Aristotle defined as a Self-Thinking-Thought and scholastic metaphysics defined as an *Ipsum Esse Subsistens* or *Ens Causa Sui*. The God of the Bible cannot be defined or proved by means of logical predictions and attributions. Even the superlatives of wisdom, power and causality advanced by medieval ontology are inadequate to the absolute otherness of God. It is not by superlatives that we can think of God, but by trying to identify the particular interhuman events which open towards transcendence and reveal the traces where God has passed. The God of ethical philosophy is not God the Almighty Being of creation, but the persecuted God of the prophets who is always in relation with man, and whose difference from man is never indifference. This is why I have tried to think of God in terms of desire, a desire that cannot be fulfilled or satisfied – in the etymological sense of *satis*, measure. I can never have enough in my relation to God for he always exceeds my measure, remains forever incommensurate with my desire. In this sense, our desire for God is without end or term: it is interminable and infinite because God reveals himself as absence rather than presence. Love is the society of God and man, but man is happier for he has God as company whereas God has man! Furthermore, when we say that God cannot satisfy man's desire, we must add that the insatisfaction is itself sublime! What is a defect in the finite order becomes an excellence in the infinite order. In the infinite order, the absence of God is better than his presence; and the anguish of man's concern and searching for God is better than consummation or comfort. As Kierkegaard put it: 'The need for God is a sublime happiness.'

Your analysis of God as an impossibility of Being or being-present would seem to suggest that the ethical relation is entirely utopian and unrealistic.

This is the great objection to my thought. 'Where did you ever see the ethical relation practised?', people say to me. I reply that its being utopian does not prevent it from investing our everyday actions of generosity or goodwill towards the other: even the smallest and most commonplace gestures, such as saying 'after you' as we sit at the dinner table or walk through a door, bear witness to the ethical. This concern for the other remains utopian in the sense that it is always 'out of place' (*u-topos*) in this world, always other than the 'ways of the world'; but there are many examples of it in the world. I remember meeting once with a group of Latin American students, well versed in the terminology of Marxist liberation and terribly concerned by the suffering and unhappiness of their people in Argentina. They asked me rather impatiently if I had ever actually witnessed the utopian rapport with the other which my ethical philosophy speaks of. I replied: 'Yes, indeed, here in this room.'

So you would maintain that Marxism bears witness to a utopian inspiration?

When I spoke of the overcoming of Western ontology as an 'ethical and prophetic cry' in 'Dieu et la philosophie' (*De Dieu qui vient à l'idée*), I was in fact thinking of Marx's critique of Western idealism as a project to understand the world rather than to transform it. In Marx's critique we find an ethical conscience cutting through the ontological identification of truth with an ideal intelligibility and demanding that theory be converted into a concrete praxis of concern for the other. It is this revelatory and prophetic cry which explains the extraordinary attraction which the Marxist utopia exerted over numerous generations. Marxism was, of course, utterly compromised by Stalinism. The 1968 Revolt in Paris was a revolt of sadness, because it came after the Khruschev Report and the exposure of the corruption of the Communist Church. The year of 1968 epitomized the joy of despair; a last grasping at human justice, happiness and perfection after the truth had dawned that the communist ideal had degenerated into totalitarian bureaucracy. By 1968 only dispersed groups and rebellious pockets of individuals remained to seek their surrealist forms of salvation, no longer confident in a collective movement of humanity, no longer assured that Marxism could survive the Stalinist catastrophe as the prophetic messenger of history.

> What role can philosophy serve today? Has it in fact reached that end which so many contemporary continental philosophers have spoken of?

It is true that philosophy, in its traditional forms of ontotheology and logocentrism – to use Heidegger's and Derrida's terms – has come to an end. But it is not true of philosophy in the other sense of critical speculation and interrogation. The speculative practice of philosophy is by no means near its end. Indeed the whole contemporary discourse of overcoming and deconstructing metaphysics is far more speculative in many respects than metaphysics itself. Reason is never so versatile as when it puts itself in question. In the contemporary end of philosophy, philosophy has found a new lease of life.

Select bibliography of Emmanuel Lévinas

La Théorie de l'intuition dans la phénoménologie de Husserl, Vrin, Paris, 1930.

De l'existence à l'existant, Vrin, Paris, 1947.

En découvrant l'existence avec Husserl et Heidegger, Vrin, Paris, 1949.

Totalité et infini. Essai sur l'extériorité, Nijhoff, La Haye, 1961; English translation, *Totality and Infinity*, transl. Alphonso Lingis, Duquesne University Press, Pittsburgh, Pa, 1969.

Difficile liberté, Albin Michel, Paris, 1963.

Quatre lectures talmudiques, Editions de Minuit, Paris, 1968.

Humanisme de l'autre homme, Fata Morgana, Montpellier, 1972.

Autrement qu'être, ou au-delà de l'essence, Nijhoff, La Haye, 1974; English translation, *Otherwise than Being, or beyond Essence*, transl. Alphonso Lingis, Nijhoff, The Hague, 1981.

Noms propres, Fata Morgana, Montpellier, 1975.

Du sacré au Saint. Cinq nouvelles talmudiques, Editions de Minuit, Paris, 1977.

Le Temps et l'Autre, Fata Morgana, Montpellier, 1979.

L'Au-delà du verset. Lectures et discours talmudiques, Editions de Minuit, Paris, 1982.

De Dieu qui vient à l'idée, Vrin, Paris, 1982.

Herbert Marcuse

Prefatory note

Herbert Marcuse was born in Berlin in 1898 to a prosperous family of assimilated Jews. While still a youth he became an active member of the Social Democratic Party. It was only after the failure of the German Revolution in 1919 that Marcuse decided to devote himself to the study of aesthetics and philosophy, first in Berlin, then in Freiburg in 1929, where he submitted his doctoral thesis on Hegel's *Concept of History* and worked under both Husserl and Heidegger. Fleeing from Nazi Germany in the early thirties, Marcuse became a close associate of Max Horkheimer's Institute for Social Research (exiled from Frankfurt), which sought to apply the dialectical theories of Hegel and Marx to the critique of such contemporary issues as mass culture, anti-Semitism, Enlightenment positivism, authoritarianism and fascism. His work with the Institute brought him into contact with Lukacs, Fromm, Benjamin, Adorno and other humanist Marxist thinkers. It was in this middle period of his intellectual career that Marcuse launched a radical project to explore socio-cultural models of liberation as alternatives to the extremes of consumer capitalism and totalitarian communism. After the war, Marcuse worked at both Columbia and Harvard on a critical analysis of Soviet Marxism (published in 1958). In the late fifties, sixties and seventies he taught at Brandeis University in Boston, *l'Ecole des Hautes Etudes* in Paris, and the University of California; and it was during this mature period that he developed and refined his multifaceted critique of advanced industrial societies, a highly influential analysis which proved a seminal source of ideas for New Left thinking. Marcuse died in 1978.

Though never claiming to be an original thinker in the strict sense of the words, Marcuse's work was singularly representative in that it provided a critical synthesis of three of the major movements of modern Continental thought: (1) the *phenomenological* movement inaugurated by Husserl and Heidegger to which the young Marcuse contributed as a research student in Freiburg (1928–32); (2) the *dialectical* movement of Hegelian Marxism, tailored by the rationalist humanism of the German Idealist tradition, which Marcuse espoused as a member of the Frankfurt School of Social Research after 1933; (3) the *psychoanlytic* movement based on a Freudian meta-psychology of unconscious drives which Marcuse refashioned in the sixties into a critique of the repressive strategies of contemporary culture.

Perhaps the keynote of Marcuse's philosophy was its insistence that the relation of modern thought and ideology to modern society be critically investigated. Hence the use of the term 'critical social theory' to characterize his thought. Marcuse's critical theory exerted a widespread influence on both the Continental and Anglo-American worlds of contemporary philosophical debate. His exile in the United States provided Marcuse with the opportunity to introduce some of the most significant modern European thinkers – particularly Hegel, Marx, Freud and Heidegger – to an English-speaking academia still largely conditioned by the 'one-dimensional' methodologies of behaviourism, positivism and common-sense empiricism. Since the forties, Marcuse's principal works – *Reason and Revolution* (1941), *Eros and Civilization* (1955), *One-dimensional Man* (1964), and *Counter-revolution and Revolt* (1972) – were published in both English and German and served to conflate the author's critical responses to both cultures. One conspicuous result of this convergence was the manner in which Marcuse's critique of advanced technological cultures and his dovetailing of political and aesthetic discourse were able to function as a guiding inspiration for the 1968 student revolts in both the United States and Europe.

Marcuse's most significant contribution to contemporary thinking was undoubtedly his ability to combine the concerns of a formalist aesthetics of subjective transcendence with a liberal revolutionary politics. Indeed one of his first projects in the early thirties was to try to reconcile an existentialist hermeneutics of subjectivity with a Marxist–Hegelian dialectics of history. And throughout his works, one finds an unswerving emphasis on the capacity of critical individuals for free aesthetic consciousness and revolutionary praxis combined with a systematic critique of the technological domination and dehumanization of contemporary 'one-dimensional' societies, East and West.

The dialogue that follows took place in San Diego, California, in 1976, two years before Marcuse's death.

*The Philosophy of art and politics**

Richard Kearney: As a Marxist thinker of international renown and inspirational mentor of student revolutions in both the United States and Europe in the sixties, you have puzzled many by the turn to primarily aesthetic questions in your recent works. How would you wish to explain or justify the turn?

Herbert Marcuse: It seems to have become quite evident that the advanced industrial countries have long since reached the stage of wealth and productivity which Marx projected for the construction of a socialist society. Consequently, a quantitative increase in material productivity is now seen to be insufficient in itself, and a qualitative change in society as a whole is seen to be necessary. Such a qualitative change presupposes, of course, new and unalienating conditions of labour, distribution and living, but that *alone* is not enough. The qualitative change necessary to build a truly socialist society, something we haven't yet seen, depends on other values – not so much economic (quantitative) as aesthetic (qualitative) in character. This change in turn requires more than just a gratification of needs; it requires, in addition, a change in the nature of these needs themselves. This is why the Marxian revolution in our age must look to art also, if it is to succeed.

If art, then, is to play such a central role in the revolutionary transition to a new society, why didn't Marx himself say that?

*A shortened version of this dialogue appeared in *The Crane Bag Journal of Irish Studies* (edited by Richard Kearney and Mark Hederman), vol. 1, no. 1, 1977.

Marx did not say that, because Marx lived over a hundred years ago and so did not write in an age when, as I have just maintained, the problems of the material culture could in fact be resolved by the establishment of genuinely socialist institutions and relationships. Consequently, he did not fully realize that a purely economic resolution of the problem can never be enough, and so lacked the insight that a twentieth-century revolution would require a different type of human being and that such a revolution would have to aim at, and, if successful, implement, an entirely new set of personal and sexual relationships, a new morality, a new sensibility and a total reconstruction of the environment. These are, to a great extent, aesthetic values (aesthetic to be understood in the larger sense of our sensory and imaginative culture which I outlined in *Eros and Civilization*, following Kant and Schiller), and that is why I think that one viewing the possibility of struggle and change in our time recognizes the decisive role which art must play.

> You spoke there, rather dangerously it seems to me, about the possible necessity of 'implementing' these new personal relationships, etc., which would characterize the qualitatively new society. How can art or culture be instrumental in this implementation without becoming the tool of some dictatorial elite (which would see it as its role to determine what should be 'implemented') and without, consequently, degenerating into propaganda?

Art can never and never should become *directly* and immediately a factor of political praxis. It can only have effect *indirectly*, by its impact on the consciousness and on the subconsciousness of human beings.

> You are saying therefore that art must always maintain a critical and *negative* detachment from the realm of everyday political practice?

Yes, I would claim that all authentic art is *negative*, in the sense that it refuses to obey the established reality, its language, its order, its conventions and its images. As such, it can be negative in two ways: *either* in so far as it serves to give asylum or refuge to defamed humanity and thus preserves in another form an alternative to the 'affirmed' reality of the establishment; *or* in so far as it serves to negate this 'affirmed' reality by denouncing both it and the defamers of humanity who have affirmed it in the first place.

> Is it not true, however, that in many of your writings (I think particularly of *Essay on Liberation* and *Eros and Civilization*) you suggest that art can play a more directly political and indeed *positive* role, by helping to point the way to a socialist utopia?

Art can give you the 'images' of a freer society and of more human relationships but beyond that it cannot go. In this sense, the difference between aesthetic and political theory remains unbridgeable: Art can say what it wants to say only in terms of the complete and formal fate of individuals in their struggle with their society in the medium of *sensibility*; its images are felt and imagined rather than intellectually formulated or propounded, whereas political theory is necessarily *conceptual*.

> How then would you view the role of reason in art – I refer not to '*Verstand*' (reason in the narrow enlightenment sense of strictly logical, mathematical and empirico-metric calculation) but to the larger Kantian and Hegelian concept of '*Vernunft*' (reason in the larger sense, which is the critical and regulative faculty of man) concerned primarily with those realms of human perception, intuition, evaluation and ethical deliberation so central, it would seem, to the concerns of any cultural aesthetic?

I believe that you cannot have the liberation of human sensitivity and sensibility without a corresponding liberation of the rational faculty (*Vernunft*) of man. Any liberation effected by art signifies therefore, a liberation of both the senses and reason from their present servitude.

> Would you be opposed then to the emotionally euphoric and Dionysian character of much of contemporary popular culture – rock music, for example?

I am wary of all exhibitions of free-wheeling emotionalism and as I explained in *Counter-revolution and Revolt*, I think that both the 'living' theatre movement (the attempt to bring theatre out into the street and make it 'immediate' by 'tuning in' to the language and sentiments of the working class) and the 'rock' cult are prone to this error. The former, despite its noble struggle, is ultimately self-defeating. It tries to blend the theatre and the revolution, but ends up blending a contrived immediacy with a clever brand of mystical humanism. The latter, the 'rock-group' cult, seems open to the danger of a form of commercial totalitarianism which absorbs the individual into an uninhibited mass where the power of a collective unconscious is mobilized but left without any radical or critical awareness. It could, at times, prove a dangerous outburst of irrationalism.

Accepting the fact, then, that a revolutionary liberation of the senses requires also a liberation of reason, the question still remains as to who is to decide what is rational, what criteria, in turn, are to be deployed in such a decision and also, who is consequently to endorse and implement this rational liberation? In other words, how do you obviate the unsavoury prospect of a benevolent, 'rational' dictator or elite imposing their criteria on the manipulated and 'irrational' masses?

The aesthetic liberation of the rational and sensible faculties (at present repressed) will have to begin with individuals and small groups, trying, as it were, such an experiment in unalienated living. How it then gradually becomes effective in terms of the society at large and makes for a different construction of social relationships in general, we cannot say. Such premature programming could only lead to yet another example of ideological tyranny.

Would you then disagree with your former colleague, Walter Benjamin, when he urges that popular culture, and particularly the cinema (which he held enables the critical and receptive attitudes of the public to coincide) be used in a politically committed fashion to aid and abet the socialist revolution?

Yes, I would have to disagree with Benjamin there. Any attempt to use art to effect a 'mass' conversion of sensibility and consciousness is inevitably an abuse of its true functions.

Its true functions being. . .?

Its true functions being (1) to negate our present society, (2) to anticipate the trends of future society, (3) to criticize destructive or alienating trends, and (4) to suggest 'images' of creative and unalienating ones.

> And this fourfold function of *negation*, *anticipation*, *critique* and *suggestion* would presumably be aimed at the individual or small group?

Yes, that is correct.

> Would you wish to retract your allegiance to the Frankfurt School's Marxist aesthetic as expressed in the following formulation: 'We interpret art as a kind of a code language for processes taking place within society which must be deciphered by means of critical analysis'?

Yes, that seems to me to be too reductive. Art is more than a code or puzzle which would 'reflect' the world in terms of a second-order aesthetic structure. Art is not just a mirror. It can never only imitate reality. Photography does that much better. Art has to transform reality so that it appears in the light (1) of what it does to human beings, and (2) of the possible images of freedom and happiness, which it might provide for these same human beings; and this is something photography cannot do. Art, therefore, does not just mirror the present, it leads beyond it. It preserves, and thus allows us to remember, values which are no longer to be found in our world; and it points to another possible society in which these values may be realized. Art is a code only to the extent that it acts as a mediated critique of society. But it cannot as such be a direct or immediate indictment of society – that is the work of theory and politics.

> Would you not say that the works of Orwell, Dickens, or the French Surrealists, for example, were directly or immediately an indictment of their society?

Well, the Surrealists were never, it seems to me, *directly* political; Orwell was not a great writer; and Dickens, like all great writers, was far more than a political theorist; reading him gives us positive pleasure and thereby ensures that there is a reader for the book in the first place. This is one of the central dilemmas of art conceived as an agent of revolution. Even the most radical art cannot, in its denunciation of the evils of society, dispense with the element of entertainment. That is why Bertolt Brecht always maintained that even the work which most brutally depicts what is going on in the world must also please. And one additional point to be remembered here is that even when certain works of art *appear* directly social or political in *content*, e.g. Orwell and Dickens, but also Zola, Ibsen, Buchner, Delacroix, Picasso, etc., they are never so in *form*, for the work always remains committed to the structure of art, to the form of the novel, drama, poem and painting, etc. and thereby testifies to a distance from reality.

What is your opinion then of the notion of a 'proletarian' art?

I think it is false for several reasons. Its attempt to transcend the distancing forms of classical and romantic art and to unite art and reality by providing in their stead a 'living art' to 'anti-art' rooted in the actions, slang and spontaneous sensations of the oppressed folk, seems to me to be doomed to failure, as I have argued in *Counterrevolution and Revolt*. Although in earlier works I stressed the political potential of the linguistic rebellion of the blacks witnessed in their folk music, dance and particularly language (whose very obscenity I interpreted as a legitimate protest against their misery and repressed cultural tradition), I now believe that such a potential is ultimately ineffective, for it has become standardized and can no longer be identified as the expression of frustrated radicals, but all too often as the futile gratification of aggressiveness which too easily turns against sexuality itself. (For instance, the 'obligatory' verbalization of the genital sphere in 'radical' speech has not been a political threat to the Establishment so much as a debasement of sexuality, e.g. if some radical exclaims, 'Fuck Nixon', he is associating the term for the highest gratification with the highest member of the oppressive Establishment!)

What is your view of 'living' or 'natural' music which has always been associated with the oppressed classes in the West and particularly with the black culture?

Well, it seems to me that here again one finds the same thing occurring. What originally started out as an authentic cry and song of the oppressed black community has since been transformed and commercialized into 'white' rock, which, by means of contrived 'performances', serves as an orgiastic group therapy which removes all the frustrations and inhibitions of the audiences, but only *temporarily* and without any socio-political foundation.

> I take it then that you would not support the idea of an art of the masses, an art devoted to the working-class struggle?

No, it seems to me that rather than being a particular code of the struggle of the proletariat or working class, art can transcend any *particular* class interest without eliminating such an interest. It is always concerned with history but history is the history of *all* classes. And it is this generality which accounts for that universal validity and objectivity of art which Marx called the quality of 'prehistory' and which Hegel called the 'continuity of substance' from the beginning of art to the end – the truth which links the modern novel and the medieval epic, the facts and possibilities of human existence, conflict and reconciliation between man and man, man and nature. A work of art will obviously contain a class content (to the extent to which it reflects the values, situations and sentiments of a feudal, bourgeois or proletarian world view) but it becomes transparent as the condition of the universal dreams of humanity. Authentic art never *merely* acts as a mirror of a class or as an 'automatic', spontaneous outburst of its frustrations and desires. The very 'sensuous immediacy' which art expresses, presupposes, however surreptitiously (and this is something which most of our popular culture has forgotten), a complex, disciplined and formal synthesis of experience according to certain universal principles which alone can lend to the work more than a purely private significance. It is because of this 'universal' dimension of art that some of the greatest political radicals have displayed the most apolitical stances and tastes in art (e.g. the famous sympathizers of the Paris Commune of 1871, or even Marx himself). Many of the apparently *formless* works of modern art (those of Cage, Stockhausen, Beckett or Ginsberg) are in fact highly intellectual, constructivist and *formal*. And indeed this fact hints, I believe, at the passing of anti-art and the return to *form*. It is because of this 'universal' significance of art as form that we may find the meaning of revolution better expressed in Bertolt Brecht's most perfect lyrics than in his explicitly political polemics; or in Bob Dylan's most 'soulful' and deeply personal songs rather than in his propagandist manifestos. Both Brecht and Dylan have one message: to make an end with things as they are. Even in the event of a total absence of political content, their works can invoke, for a vanishing moment, the image of a liberated world and the pain of an alienated one. Thus, the aesthetic dimension assumes a political and revolutionary value, but without becoming the mouthpiece of any particular class interest.

> A certain detachment from the political reality would seem then almost prerequisite for a genuinely revolutionary art, would it not?

Yes, art must always remain alienated to some extent and this precludes an identification of art with revolutionary praxis. As I argued in *Counter-revolution and Revolt*, art cannot represent the revolution, it can only invoke it in another medium, in an aesthetic structure in which the political content becomes *meta*political, governed by the formal necessity of art. And so the goal of all revolution – a world of tranquillity and freedom – can appear in a totally unpolitical medium under the aesthetic laws of beauty and harmony.

> Would it be fair to conclude, therefore, that you reject the various attempts by Lenin, Lukacs and other Marxist dialecticians to formulate the possibility of *progressive art* as a weapon of class war?

The belief that only a 'proletarian' literature can fulfil the progressive function of art and develop a revolutionary consciousness seems to me a mistaken one in our age. Today the working class shares the same world view and values as those of a large part of other classes, especially the middle class. The conditions and goals of a revolution against global monopoly capitalism today cannot therefore be adequately articulated in terms of a proletarian revolution; and so if this revolution is to be present in some way as a goal in art, such art could not be typically proletarian. Indeed, it seems to me more than a matter of personal preference that both Lenin and Trotsky were critical of the notion of a 'proletarian culture'. But even if you could argue for a 'proletarian culture', you would still be left asking whether there is such a thing as a proletariat (as Marx described it) in our age. In the United States, for example, one finds that the working people are often apathetic if not totally hostile to socialism, while in Italy and France, strongholds of the Marxist tradition of labour, the workers seem to be ruled by a Communist Party and trade unionism manipulated very often by the USSR and committed to the minimum strategy of compromise or tolerance. In both situations, that is, in the US and in Europe, it would seem that a large part of the working class has become a class of bourgeois society, and their 'proletarian' socialism, if it exists at all, no longer appears as a definitive negation of capitalism. Consequently, the attempt to turn the emotions of the working class into a standard for authentic radical and socialist art is a regressive step and can only result in a superficial adjustment of the established order, and a perpetuation of the prevailing 'atmosphere' of oppression and alienation. For instance, authentic 'black literature' is revolutionary but it is not a 'class' literature as such, and its *particular* content is at the same time a *universal* one. One finds here in the particular situation of an alienated radical minority the most 'universal' of all needs: the need of the individual and his group to exist as *human* beings.

> We seem to have returned again to the notion of 'aesthetic' revolution as something centred around individuals and small groups in its advocation of and experimentation with unalienated living. Are you in fact suggesting that it might be possible for certain individuals and small groups to live in a non-alienated manner in an alienated world? (I think here in particular of certain dissenting artists, intellectuals, ecologists, anti-nuclear pacifists, or the advocates of alternative modes of co-operative or community existence.)

No. One cannot actually *live* in a non-alienated manner in an alienated world. You can *experiment* with it, you can *remember* it; you can in your own little circle try your best to develop it, but beyond that you cannot go.

> Would you agree that it is by means of the aesthetic imagination that one can transcend one's alienated world, in order to 'experiment' with and 'remember' alternative forms of life as you suggest?

Yes, that is correct, and imaginative remembrance is particularly important, for it is by remembering the values and desires which, unable over the ages to express themselves in a politically corrupt world, took refuge in art and thus preserved themselves, that we shall be able to find hints of a direction out of our present alienation.

This notion of art as hinting at a new direction would seem to me to be a *positive* one; but have you not already on many occasions, and even in this interview, confirmed the view, held by Brecht, Beckett and Kafka, to name but a few, that art must be *negative* ('estranged') and 'alienating' if it is to remain authentic?

Yes, indeed, I did and still do support that view. Art must never lose its negative and alienating power, for it is there that its most radical potential lies. To lose this 'negating' power is, in effect, to eliminate the tension between art and reality, and so also the very real distinctions between subject and object, quantity and quality, freedom and servitude, beauty and ugliness, good and evil, future and present, justice and injustice, etc. Such a claim to a final synthesis of these historical oppositions in the here and now would be the materialist version of absolute idealism. It would signal a state of perfect barbarism at the height of civilization. In other words, to do away with these distinctions between value and fact is to deny present reality and forestall our search for another more human one. Indeed, the common negative force of a piece of music by Verdi and Bob Dylan, a piece of writing by Flaubert and Joyce or a painting by Ingres and Picasso is precisely that hint of beauty which acts as refusal of the commodity world and of the performances, attitudes, looks and sounds required by it.

So the artistic imagination, you would say, can in no way be revolutionary in a 'positive' sense?

Art, as we know it, cannot transform reality and cannot, therefore, submit to the actual requirements of the revolution without denying itself. It is only as a negative and alienating power that it can in fact negate, dialectically, the alienation of the political reality. And, as such, as the negation of the negation, to use Hegel's term, it is indeed revolutionary. That is why in *Counter-revolution and Revolt* and elsewhere I described the relation between art and politics as a unity of opposites, an antagonistic unity which must always remain antagonistic.

In *Essay on Liberation*, you speak at one point about technology being used by the revolutionary in the same way as the painter uses his canvas and brush. Does not this analogy suggest a direct and positive relationship to the socio-political reality?

In some limited sense I suppose it does. It is true, I believe, that technology should, ideally, be used creatively and imaginatively to reconstruct nature and the environment.

> But according to what criteria?

According to the criterion of beauty.

> But who decides this criterion? Is it universal for all men and women? And if so, in what way does it, as an 'aesthetic' criterion, differ from a theological or ontological system of value?

I think that the striving for beauty is simply an essential part of human sensibility.

> But surely, if our world is to undergo a revolutionary reconstruction in the name of and for the sake of beauty, one must be quite sure in advance what this 'beauty' is – whether it is in fact the universal and absolute goal of all human striving, or merely the subjective and particular goal of one revolutionary leader/artist or an elite of revolutionary leaders/artists? If the latter, then how does one deny the charge of totalitarian imposition, manipulation and tyranny?

A revolution cannot be waged for the sake of beauty. Beauty is but one criterion which plays a leading role in one element of the revolution, i.e. the restoration and reconstruction of the environment. It cannot be used to 'reconstruct' men without, as you correctly infer, running the risk of totalitarianism. It simply cannot presume to go that far.

> In *Eros and Civilization* it certainly seems, however, as if you are suggesting that 'beauty' is no less than the ultimate end or *telos* of all human struggle; and that this teleological struggle is itself synonymous with Freud's 'meta-psychological' interpretation of 'eros' or Kant's view that 'all aesthetic endeavor seeks beauty as its final purpose'.

No. Beauty is only one amongst other goals.

> You would not wish then in any sense to ascribe an absolute character to beauty?

No, beauty can never be absolute. Nevertheless, I think that certain evaluative criteria can be established in relation to it.

How then would you react to Martin Jay's assertion in his book on the Frankfurt School, entitled *The Dialectical Imagination*, that your repeated attempts to describe man's desire for an ideal utopia are rooted in the latent Judeo-Messianic optimism of the Frankfurt School, which, in fact, consisted almost exclusively of German Jewish intellectuals, e.g. Adorno, Fromm, Horkheimer, Benjamin and of course, yourself, who wished to synthesize the intuitions of two other Jews, Marx and Freud?

I do not recall on any occasion having described or even attempted to describe such a thing as utopia. The relationships which I indicate as essential for qualitative change are certainly 'aesthetic', but they are not utopian.

So you would deny any link between your political optimism about a new society and the Messianic optimism of Judaism?

Absolutely.

Another current interpretation of the continual striving for universal and objective value-criteria in your recent writings on the 'aesthetic revolution' is that you are in fact returning, albeit surreptitiously, to the 'fundamental ontology' of your original mentor, Martin Heidegger – seeking a new kind of 'poetic dwelling on earth'. Do you see your later works as a return to your early attempts in the thirties to reconcile a Heideggerean phenomenology of subjective historicity and a Marxist dialectics of collective history?

That Heidegger had a profound influence on me is without any doubt, and I have never denied it. He taught me a great deal about what real phenomenological 'thinking' is, about how thinking is not just a logical function of 'representing' what *is*, here and now in the present, but operates at deeper levels in its 'recalling' of what has been forgotten and its 'projecting' what might yet come to pass in the future. That appreciation of the temporal and intentional nature of phenomena has been extremely important for me, but that is as far as it goes.

Evidently art has, in your opinion, a radical role to play in detaching individuals from their mindless slavery to the present conditions of work, competition, performance, advertising, mass media, etc., and thereby educating them in their own reality. Indeed, you have spoken very often of late about *art as education*. Would you like to briefly comment on this relationship?

Such an education in the reality of one's repressed faculties – sensory, imaginative and rational – and in our repressive environmental and working conditions would have to be based not on a mass education plan (that again would be to abuse art by turning it into propaganda) but in small communal projects of *auto-critique*. Such auto-critique would not, of course, replace a general education. It could not be a question of substituting one for the other, of abandoning the traditional tools of education altogether; not so much a question of *deschooling* as *reschooling*.

Such an 'aesthetic' reschooling, which as you say would not be alternative, but supplementary to a general basic education, would presumably be concerned with those ethical and existential areas of human relations which constitute the locus of a *qualitative* leap to another society, would it not?

Yes it would.

And presumably you would like to be able to base such an aesthetic education on certain universal principles whose objectivity would preclude the danger of an ideological indoctrination of the 'ignorant' and 'gullible' masses by some 'enlightened' elite: an abuse of education which is directly conducive to totalitarianism and fascism.

Yes, that is certainly a very real danger. And in order to be as objective as possible, one must try to determine objectively what are the seats of power today and how they influence what they have established as reality. This objectivity would then be based on what is the reality of our present society and not on ideological constructions.

But I suspect that in your projection of the 'images' of a new society you tend to go behind an objectivity founded in *what is*, to an objectivity founded in *what ought to be*; and so we return to the old question: what is this 'ought' which would govern the aesthetic transformation of human beings and their relations with one another?

There is no such thing as an absolute prescriptive criterion for change. If a man is happy in the society in which he presently finds himself, then he has condemned himself. This problem has never bothered me. A human being who today still thinks that the world ought not to be changed is below the level of discussion. I have no problems about the 'is' and the 'ought'; it is a problem invented by philosophers.

> But if the question is so unproblematical, what is it that separates man's desire for a freer and unalienated society from the animal's? I mean, why doesn't an animal feel the imperative need to change its world into a qualitatively better one?

It cannot, but it does at least have enough instinct to realize that when its environment is lacking in food, warmth and a mate it must migrate to another.

> How then would you account for the difference between man's desire to change his world and the animal's desire to change his?

An animal has no reason whereas a human being has and so can outline, indirectly by means of art and directly by means of political theory, *possible* directions for future improvement.

> Man, therefore, would seem by virtue of his reason (*Vernunft*) to possess some universal orientation towards a future society – something which you frequently spoke of in your early writings – which the animal does not possess. But by viewing man's rational imagination in this way, as a power capable of transcending the immediate continuum of history, and of projecting alternative possibilities for a future society, you would seem once again, would you not, to have moved beyond the strictly empirical realm of the 'is'? How would you account then for this exigency, so manifest in the passions of artists and intellectuals, to transcend the given mores and conventions of our present society in search of new and better ones?

Everyone searches for something better. Everyone searches for a society in which there is no more alienated labour. There is no need for a guiding principle or goal; it is simply a matter of common sense.

Would you wish to equate the striving for beauty and the ideal society with the abolition of alienated labour?

Of course not. Once the problem of alienated labour is solved there will be many others which remain. The creative and imaginative faculties of man will never be redundant. If art is something which among other things can point to the 'images' of a political utopia, it is inevitably something which can never cease to be. Art and politics will never finally coalesce because the ideal society which art strives for in its negation of all alienated societies presupposes an ideal reconciliation of opposites, which can never be achieved in any absolute or Hegelian sense. The relationship between art and political praxis is therefore dialectical. As soon as one problem is solved in a synthesis, new problems are born and so the process continues without end. The day when men try to identify opposites in an ultimate sense, thus ignoring the inevitable rupture between art and revolutionary praxis, will sound the death-knell for art. Man must never cease to be an artist, to criticize and negate his present self and society and to project by means of his creative imagination alternative 'images' of existence. He can never cease to imagine for he can never cease to change.

Select bibliography of Herbert Marcuse

Hegels Ontologie und die Grundlegung einer Theorie der Geschichtlichkeit, V. Klostermann, Frankfurt, 1932.

Reason and Revolution: Hegel and the Rise of Social Theory, Oxford University Press, New York, 1941.

Eros and Civilization: a Philosophical Inquiry into Freud, Beacon Press, Boston, 1955.

Soviet Marxism: a Critical Analysis, Columbia University Press, New York, 1958.

One-dimensional Man: Studies in the Ideology of Advanced Industrial Society, Beacon Press, Boston, 1964.

Kultur und Gesellschaft, Suhrkamp, Frankfurt, 1965.

Das Ende der Utopie, Maikowski, West Berlin, 1967.

Psychoanalyse und Politik, Europäische, Frankfurt, 1968.

An Essay on Liberation, Beacon Press, Boston, 1969.

Ideen zu einer kritischen Theorie der Gesellschaft, Suhrkamp, Frankfurt, 1969.

Five Lectures, Beacon Press, Boston, 1970.

Counter-revolution and Revolt, Beacon Press, Boston, 1972.

Studies in Critical Philosophy, Beacon Press, Boston, 1973.

Revolution or Reform? A Confrontation, Afterword by Franz Stark, New University Press, Chicago, 1976.

Gespräche mit Herbert Marcuse, Suhrkamp, Frankfurt, 1978.

The Aesthetic Dimension: Toward a Critique of Marxist Aesthetics, Beacon Press, Boston, 1978.

Schriften, I: Der deutsche Künstlerroman/Frühe Aufsätz, Suhrkamp, Frankfurt, 1978.

Schriften, 3: Aufsätze aus der Zeitschrift für Sozialforschung, 1934–1941, Suhrkamp, Frankfurt, 1979.

Schriften, 5: Triebstruktur und Gesellschaft: Ein philosophischer Beitrag zu Sigmund Freud, transl. Marianne von Eckhardt-Jaffe, Suhrkamp, Frankfurt, 1979. This volume is a translation of *Eros and Civilization: a Philosophical Inquiry into Freud* (see above).

Stanislas Breton

Prefatory note

Stanislas Breton was born in Gironde, France, in 1912. While still in his teens, he joined the Passionist order of Catholic priests. Accordingly, his early philosophical schooling was deeply influenced by the Thomistic and scholastic traditions, as well, he insists, as by his childhood experiences of nature in rural France. This formative dual fidelity to the immanence of finite being and the transcendence of an infinite God expressed itself in his first published work in 1951, *L'esse* in *et l'esse* ad *dans la métaphysique de la relation*. Moreover, this central relationship between the claims of immanence and transcendence, appropriation and disappropriation, habitation and exodus also profoundly determined his interpretation of phenomenology, which he discovered after the war, and particularly the key notion of 'intentionality' as a dynamic movement of consciousness beyond the self towards what is *other* (*Approches phénoménologiques de l'idée d'être*, 1959, and *Etre, monde, imaginaire*, 1976).

The main body of Breton's writings have focused on contemporary philosophy, and especially on the ways in which the contemporary theories of phenomenology, logic and mathematics help us to reinterpret the ontologies of neoplatonism and Thomism (see *Essence et existence*, 1962; *Situation de la philosophie contemporaine*, 1959; *Saint Thomas d'Aquin*, 1965; *Philosophie et mathematiques chez Proclus*, 1969; *Du principe*, 1971). In addition to these philosophical studies, however, Breton has published a number of influential works on more specifically religious and mystical subjects, such as *La Passion du Christ et les philosophies* (1954), *Mystique de la Passion* (1962), *Foi et raison logique* (1971) and *Théories des idéologies* (1976).

A further dimension of his thought has been a pioneering attempt to build bridges not only between the rival traditions of Greek ontology and Judeo-Christian theology, but also between the modern movement of religious philosophy and radical political theory – in particular that of Marxism.

Common to Breton's three major intellectual concerns – ontology, religion and politics – is his insistence on the indispensable necessity of a critical disposition, what he calls '*l'opérateur de transcendance*'. This critical operation serves to expose the limitations of every form of established power, every pretence at a fixed or absolute determination, forever redirecting us towards the possibility of an elsewhere; it consists, writes Breton in *Théorie des idéologies*, in 'imagining another space in which another indeterminate possibility freely unfolds, and which demands to be *thought* even if it is impossible to be *known*'.

Having taught at the Pontifical University in Rome during the fifties, Breton returned to France to become Professor of Philosophy, first at the University of Lyons and later at the *Institut Catholique* in Paris. In 1970, he was appointed *Maître de Conférence* at *l'École Normale Supérieur*, an honour shared with Jacques Derrida and Louis Althusser, the Marxist theoretician who proposed his nomination. Breton was the first 'Catholic' philosopher to obtain this post, an indication, it would seem, of the high esteem in which he is regarded by the new generation of intellectuals on the Continent. Though few of his works have as yet been translated into English, Breton remains the most eminent Catholic thinker living in France today.

This dialogue took place at Clamart, France, in 1982.

Being, God and the poetics of relation

Richard Kearney: Your philosophical journey has been wide ranging. You have published works on such diverse topics as neoplatonism, Thomism, Marxism, phenomenology, logic and poetics. What would you consider to be the unifying threads in this tapestry of intellectual interests?

Stanislas Breton: First, I would say that my philosophical journey is related to my biographical one. My early upbringing and education in a rural community in La Vendée certainly had a significant impact on my subsequent thinking; it determined my later leanings towards a certain philosophical *realism*. This perhaps accounts somewhat for the fact that in the doctorate I presented to the Sorbonne, *Approches phénomenologiques de l'idée d'être*, I tended to see the key metaphysical concept, 'Being as Being', in terms of the four elements of the concretely experienced, real world – earth, fire, water, air. Strange as it may sound, the monastic experience of my early years in a Passionist seminary, which I entered at the age of fifteen, also corresponded in some way to my conceptualization of *Being as Being*: this decisive concept thus emerged as both a monastic desert and an all-englobing shelter of the four elements of nature. Philosophy begins, I believe, in the life-world. So it is not very surprising that our understanding of Being should be coloured by our lived experience, by the formative *images* of our being in the world. This conviction predisposed me, of course, to a *phenomenological* approach to philosophy; it also confirmed my belief that a poetics of imagination is an indispensable dimension of genuine thinking.

> I think that your conviction would be shared by many of the phenomenologists. Sartre, Camus and Merleau-Ponty all spoke of the decisive way in which their concretely *lived experience* affected their subsequent understanding of Being, which they saw as a 'universal' reflection on their 'particular', prereflective existence. But what philosophical or intellectual influences on your thinking would you consider to be of primary importance?

The earliest intellectual influence I can recall was the Latin language – the way in which it was used in the seminary with a scholastic emphasis on professorial rigour and prepositional distinctions: *ex, in, ad, de* and so on. This language of *relations*, which Lévinas calls 'transitive language', greatly influenced my doctorate in Rome entitled '*L'Esse* in *et l'esse* ad *dans la métaphysique de la relation*. This scholastic logic of relations was the second major influence on my philosophical imagination for it raised the fundamental question of how man can be *in* Being (immanence) and still be said to be moving *towards* it (transcendence). Once applied to the work of St. Thomas, it opened up the whole problematic of the 'operations' of ontological immanence with its crucial theological implications for our understanding of the Trinity: How does the Son belong to the Father and the Father to the Son through the agency of the Spirit? I would almost say that my mature interest in philosophy sprang from theological questions which theology itself could not answer. For example, the *Being-in* relation provided an explanation of the unity of the Three Persons of the Trinity, while the distinction and difference between the Three could be understood in terms of the intentional or transitive relation of the *Being-towards*. The Spirit could thus be interpreted as a twofold relation: (i) the perpetual attraction between the Father and the Son; and (ii) the power of movement and carrying-beyond (*meta-pherein*), which refuses the finite limits of proprietal possession and makes the Trinity an *infinite relation*.

This theology of operations also has important implications for our understanding of the Incarnation. The 'substantialist' theology of the Councils, which spoke of the two natures in one, seemed to me insufficient in so far as it privileged the notion of *substance* over that of *function* or *relation*. The dynamic relation of the Being-towards category struck me as being closer to the Biblical language of transitivity. God as a Being-in-itself, as an identical substance, cannot be thought by us; we can only know or speak about God in terms of His relation to us, or ours to Him.

My interest in the theology of operations soon led to an interest in the philosophy of mathematical relations. When I was captured by the Germans during the War, I had three books in my bag: Bochenski's *Elements of Mathematical Logic*, Brunschvicg's *Modality of Judgment* and Hamelin's *The Principle Elements of Representation*. Another work which deeply fascinated me at the time was Bertrand Russell's *Introduction à la philosophie mathématique*, where he outlined a sophisticated philosophy of descriptive relations. In short, what I appreciated most in these thinkers was their analysis of the operative terms of relation – prepositions such as *in, towards*, and the conjunctions *as, as-if*, which I called 'those little servants of the Lord'. I believe they are not only the indispensable accompaniment of all thought but also the secret messengers of the philosophical future.

Could you elaborate on your philosophical transition from the initial question of *Being as Being* (an ontology of the four elements of nature) to the correlative question of *Being-in* and *Being-towards* (a metaphysics of relation)?

I was drawn towards the metaphysical problematic of relations in order to try to understand not just what Being is as such, but how it relates to man or accounts for the way in which the Three Divine Persons relate to each other. The relation of Being-towards constitutes the element of metaphor or metamorphosis, that which assures the infinite movement of existence as a passing over from one phase to the next; it is that which compels us to continually alter our concepts, making each one of us a 'being in transit'.

The relation of Being-in, by contrast, is that *élément neutre* which draws together and unifies existence; it is that which founds our notion of ontological self-identity. In the *Metaphysics*, Aristotle refers to this principle when he states that the addition of Being or the One to something changes nothing. Being added to man adds nothing. For Being is not a predicate but the most essential, necessary and universal function of existence: the function which allows each thing to be itself, to be one and the same. The principle of Being-in is that which freely grants each thing the permission to *be*, to rest and recollect itself from the movement of becoming.

Do you see this Greek metaphysics of relation radicalizing our understanding of the Judeo-Christian tradition?

I believe that both metaphysical relations – the Being-towards and the Being-in – are equally essential for an understanding of Judeo-Christian theology. At this level, I see no great opposition between Greek and Biblical thought. What we call the historical 'meaning' of Christianity or Judaism is the tradition of interpretations that have been historically ascribed to them; and in the history of Western thinking these interpretations are inextricably related to Hellenic concepts of ontology. Between the two traditions – the Greek and the Biblical – there is a creative tension which ensures that we are never fully at our intellectual ease in either. We are inevitably committed to this philosophical exodus, this vacillation between two 'homes' of thought. We have left the home of Israel just as we have left the home of Greece. We remain homesick for both. We cannot renounce the intellectual nostalgia of this double allegiance. The Western thinker is divided from *within*.

Do you see Thomism as an attempt to bridge these two traditions in your own thought?

I consider Thomism to be the paleoancephalus of my philosophical formation. There were three areas in the work of St. Thomas which particularly preoccupied me: (1) the attempt to think God and Being together; (2) the theory of intentionality and formal objects – which I rediscovered later in Brentano and Husserl (I was especially impressed by Thomas' statement that relation consists of a certain transit or transitivity; this implies that Being is transitive and that our entire existence is a series of transitions towards the other, the loving potency which forever searches for its fulfilment in act); (3) the Thomistic definition of freedom or the free being as the being that is 'cause of itself' (*causa sui*). This third concept occupied a very important place in my thought. For something to be free thus meant that, as cause of itself, it can create something new, almost from nothing. For the thinker it offers the free possibility to open up new paths of enquiry not already charted or inscribed in the map of the world.

How did you find your way from Thomism to phenomenology?

Like most philosophers of my generation I was deeply influenced by the phenomenological movement inaugurated by Husserl and his disciples, Ingarden, Häring, Heidegger and so on. I saw the phenomenological emphasis on intentionality – the methodological investigation of how our consciousness is always intentionally directed towards something *beyond* itself – as a means of extending three of my primary intellectual concerns: (1) the logic of relations governing the activity of the human mind; (2) the dynamic teleological aspect of Thomistic metaphysics expressed in the notion of the *esse ad*; and (3) the Biblical concept of exodus. Of course, the original contribution of Husserlian phenomenology was to delineate and describe the relation of intentionality in terms of concrete experience – our everyday being-in-the-world, to ground our logical and metaphysical concepts in the lived experience of consciousness. Later, particularly in a work like *Etre, monde, imaginaire*, I tried to combine these Husserlian insights into a philosophy of intentional relations invoking a more poetic language of metaphor and metamorphosis. My aim here was to suggest how our being-in-the-world, and our understanding of this being, unfolds as a creative interplay between the *logos* of reason, which unifies, regulates, structures, and the *mythos* of poetry, symbol and myth, which is forever transcending and revising the order of *logos*. Both of these directions of consciousness – the positing power of *logos* and the differentiating power of *mythos* – are founded on an *imaginaire-rien* which I define as the universal principle of language, a superabundant play which engenders all meanings.

What would you describe as the specifically phenomenological characteristics of your work, given your early fascination for the Husserlian notion of phenomenology?

First, I would say it was through my interest in the 'metaphysics of relation' that I became interested (via Brentano, on whom I was working in my Rome lectures) in Husserlian phenomenology. In fact, the relation of intentionality, which Brentano had retrieved from medieval scholasticism and 'reactivated' for contemporary philosophical purposes, struck me as offering a very liberating understanding of meaning, irreducible both to the strictly 'logical' notion of relations current in the forties and fifties, and to the traditional ontological notion of the 'transcendental' rapports between matter and form, essence and existence, and more generally between potency and act (rapports which I preferred to call 'structural' and which were typically articulated in Hamelin's *Eléments principaux de la représentation*). In my early work *Conscience et intentionalité*, I had already projected an enlarged notion of intentionality and I well remember a discussion with Jean Beaufret (one of the first advocates of existentialist and Heideggerian phenomenology in France) in which I engaged him on the crucial question of the transition from intentionality to 'existence': a question which, it seemed to me, represented a new and deeper understanding of the concept of the *esse ad* which was to pursue me all of my life. My initial interest in phenomenology, which corresponded therefore to my keenest philosophical preoccupations, also extended to my later works, in particular *Approches phénoménologiques de l'idée d'être* and *Etre, monde, imaginaire*. Overall I would say that the most inspiring aspect of phenomenology for me was its emphasis on the *prepredicative* and prereflective dimensions of experience. Indeed it was with this precise emphasis in mind that I distinguished in *Conscience et intentionalité* between several stratifications of consciousness: intentionality as a psychological act; intentionality as a 'potency/power' (*puissance*) relating to formal objects; and a transcendental intentionality representing the opening of the soul to *Being as Being*. It is along similar lines that, in the first part of *Etre, monde, imaginaire*, I proposed an analysis of what is meant by the 'language of being' in a less rudimentary way than that proposed by scholasticism or Thomism. I must admit, however, that in my early studies in phenomenology I paid little attention to the celebrated phenomenological reduction which, in the fifties, tormented those philosophers of my generation inspired by the Husserlian 'discovery'. (It was only later, by means of my reflections on freedom, that I came to appreciate somewhat what was involved in the reduction.) In summary, I would say that for me phenomenology was an extraordinary stimulant to my thinking, serving to crystallize some of my most formative philosophical concerns and ultimately providing me with an effective method of analysing the key notions of 'passage', and 'transit' which the metaphysics of relation first impressed upon me.

> Another of your recent works, *The Theory of Ideologies*, also seems to be a variation on this theme of creative intentionality or transcendence. I'm thinking particularly of the key term of this work – the 'operator of transcendence'.

This recent critique of ideology sprang from my fundamental preoccupation with the question of the 'zero'. The zero is a conceptual or mathematical way of formulating the metaphysical idea of the quasi-nothing (*rien*), or the Christian notion of the Cross – the emptiness of the crypt where Christian thinking as a critical thinking takes its source. A genuine questioning of ideology requires such a critical distance or dis-position. Without it, one can easily be misled by dogmatic ideologies – be they political or philosophical, or ecclesiastical.

The neoplatonists also taught the importance of keeping a distance from all categories of facile objectivization. Their very definition of Being as *Eidos* or Form expresses this critical reserve. They realized that our philosophical categories are really *figures* of thought, and are thus capable of being critically altered or transcended towards the truth of the One which is beyond all the forms and figures of established ontology. So that when the neoplatonists spoke of the One or God, they spoke of it in terms of critical reserve or qualification: *hos* or *oion*, *quasi* or *quatenus* – God *as* this or that ontological form. In short, since the Divine One was considered to be 'beyond being', He could only be thought of *as* being, or *as if* He were being. One could not say: God *is* being. The critical notion of the quasi-nothing, functioning as the 'operator of transcendence', thus prevented God from being reduced to a simplified or idolatrous ontology.

This neoplatonic notion of critical distance is confirmed by the Christian notion of mystery – and particularly the practice of mystical speculation advanced by Eckhart and other Christian mystics who remained very suspicious of all ontological objectivizations of God. The model of reason demanded by metaphysical thinking must, I believe, be accompanied by a mystical appreciation for that which remains beyond the reach of this metaphysical model. This is why I always felt the need to balance the Greek fidelity to Being with a Biblical fidelity to the exodus – particularly as expressed in the Christian theology of the Passion and the Cross.

> Could you explain in more detail how your theological interpretation of the Passion as dispossession/disposition relates to the critique of contemporary ideologies? I think this is a crucial transition in your thinking and perhaps accounts for your occasional leanings towards the Marxist critique.

I believe that the Christian doctrine of dispossession can be translated into modern 'socio-political' terms as a critique of power. There is a certain correspondence between the mystical–neoplatonic critique of the Divine attributes – as an attempt to *possess* God in terms of ontological properties which would reduce His transcendence to the immanence of Being – and the Marxist critique of private property. Christianity and authentic Marxism share a common call to dispossession and a critical detachment from the prevailing order. I was always struck by the similarities between the Christian doctrine of eschatological justice where Jesus identified with the poor – 'I was naked. I was hungry. I was thirsty. I was imprisoned' (Matthew, 10:9) – and the Marxist ideal of universal justice for the dispossessed. I think that this universal 'I' of Christ – not to be confused with a transcendental or absolute Ego – which is enigmatically present in every poor or outcast person who has not yet been allowed the full humanity of justice, can find common cause with what is best in genuine Marxism. I am not saying that the two are the same. For while Christianity sponsors a categorical imperative for human justice and liberation (which certain brands of Marxism also endorse), it is not simply reducible to this imperative. While both share what Ernst Bloch called a common 'principle of hope' (*principe-espérance*), pointing towards a utopian horizon in the future, Christianity transcends the limits of historical materialism in the name of a prophetic eschatology (i.e. the Coming of the Kingdom).

The term 'Christian-Marxist' is a loaded and ambiguous one: it may serve as a *question* – with all the creative, thought-provoking tensions that genuine questioning implies – but not as a *solution*. We should remain cautious about invoking such terms uncritically as yet another ideological authority.

> How would you react to those who construe your recent work as a 'Christian atheism'?

This is a dangerous term and I would not like to be thus characterized. To refuse the attempts to possess God by reducing Him to an ontological substance or political power – that is, an ideological weapon – is not to disbelieve in God; on the contrary, I would argue that it is a way of remaining faithful to one's belief. The critical refusal of ideological theism is not a refusal of God. It implies rather that the secondary definitions of God in terms of proposition (I believe *that* God exists) or predication (God *is* this or that) must be continually brought back to their primary origin in existential belief (I believe *in* God). This existential belief involves the believer in an intentional relation with God which is perhaps best described in terms of trust and transition. The move to institutionalize this belief in an invariant corpus of dogmas, doctrines and propositions was natural, perhaps even inevitable if Christianity was to survive the vagaries and contingencies of history. But this movement of *conservation* must always be accompanied by a *critical* counter-movement which reminds us that God cannot ultimately be objectified or immobilized in ontological or institutional (i.e. anthropomorphic) structures. In a recent study entitled *Théorie des idéologies et la réponse de la foi* I tried to reflect on this problem by discussing the central implications of the term *credo* in relation to the three major movements of belief – existential, propositional and predicative – mentioned above. Religious faith begins with belief-in-God which expresses itself as an intentional being-towards-God. It involves the primary existential idioms of desire, enchantment and hope, etc. It is only subsequently that we return upon the existential level to appropriate the riches encountered in the immediacy of this original experience. Thus the second movement of faith takes place as an attempt to define and order the content and form of one's existential belief. It is as if one thus draws a golden circle around one's religious experience which one calls 'tradition' or 'heritage' or 'doctrine' and affirms *that* God exists and *that* God is good and almighty, etc. In this way the vertical arrow of our primary intentional belief becomes a reflective or recollective circle – with those on the inside calling themselves Christian and those on the outside non-Christian. I think that this second move is indispensable in that every religion requires the form of a 'society', and every society requires a specific identity and foundation. A religion that is content to be 'anything at all' very easily becomes 'nothing at all' – as indeterminate and all-inconclusive as the category of Being-as-Being. In the third movement, reflection goes beyond both the modalities of 'I believe *in*' and 'I believe *that*' to the definition of God as a *proposition in itself*: 'God *is* this or that'. Hence the intentional distance or commitment implied by the first two movements of '*I* believe' is transcended and dogmatic theology instantiates itself as a historical institution or organization. It is the duty of the religious or theistic thinker to serve such institutional belief by reminding it that its doctrines are not autonomous or eternally guaranteed but intellectual sedimentations of the original 'I believe' wherein God reveals Himself to man. This critical exigency of faithfulness to the irreducible mystery and radicality of Divine revelation is beautifully expressed in a passage in Kings I:2, where Elijah goes in search of God but discovers him not in the rocks, in the storm, in the shaking earth, nor in the fire, but in the voice of a gentle breeze as it passes through the mountain cave. God is passage not possession.

Can this critique of theistic ideology also be applied to political ideologies which constitute the objectified or impersonalized institutions of contemporary society?

I think so. But we must remember the natural and almost inevitable reasons for the emergence of ideologies. Ideology springs from the fact that there is an ontological rupture between existence and consciousness. We do not coincide with ourselves. We exist before we are conscious of our existence; and this means that our reflective consciousness is always to some extent out of joint with the existential conditions that fostered it. Freud realized this when he spoke about the gap between the conscious and the unconscious. I would say that every form of *thought* is ideology to the extent that it does not and cannot fully coincide with the *being* of which it is the thought. The existence of ideologies reminds us that there is a margin of obscurity which we can never completely recuperate or remove. The pure identification of Being and Thought – i.e. the Thought that thinks itself as Being/Being as the Self-Thinking-Thought – is the Aristotelian–Thomistic definition of Divine self-understanding that no ideology can legitimitely pretend to emulate. Human thought can never be perfectly transparent or adequate to itself. It is the role of the philosopher to challenge all ideological claims to such absolute knowledge and, by implication, to absolute power.

> You once stated: 'The cross of my faith, will it not remain this interrogation mark which ancient legend tells us is the first-born of all creation?' If your philosophy does remain this critical interrogation mark, can it ever serve as a creative affirmation? Is it not inevitably condemned to a *via negativa*?

The two aspects of philosphy – as negation and affirmation – are for me by no means incompatible. Though the critical aspect is more in evidence in contemporary thinking, including my own, I would insist that the first step in philosophy – and therefore its *sine qua non* – is a fundamental experience of wonder, curiosity, or enchantment: in short *affirmation*. My enthusiasm for philosophy began in the same way as my enthusiasm for poetry or the Bible, by *responding* to texts that sang to me. Writing retraces those paths that sing to us (*chantent*) and thus enchant (*enchantent*) us. In this sense, I see a close relationship between philosophy, theology and poetics. Philosophy never speaks to us in the abstract with a capital P; but in the engaging terms of certain chosen texts (*morceaux choisis*) – in my own case, certain texts of the pre-Socratics, Aristotle, Plato, the neoplatonists or St. Thomas, Schelling, Husserl and Heidegger. The desire to know philosophy as a totality – the Hegelian temptation to absolute knowledge – is not only dangerous but impossible; one can never reduce the infinite richness of our existential experience to the totalizing limits of Reason.

But would you not acknowledge essential differences between philosophy and poetry as modes of this *affirmation enchantée*?

The main difference between philosophy and poetry as I see it is that while both originate in an experience of enchantment which draws us and commits us to the world, philosophy is obliged, in a second movement, to critically transcend and interrogate the world, both as life-experience and poetic-experience. Philosophy thus leads a double life of residing within and without the world. Perhaps one of the greatest enigmas of philosophy is that a thinking being can serve as a chain in the historical world and yet also break free from this chain, rise above it (partially at least) in order to question its ultimate origin and meaning. Poetry celebrates *that* the world exists; philosophy asks *why* the world exists. Schelling and Husserl implicitly acknowledged this distinction when they spoke of the philosophical need to go beyond or suspend the natural attitude (which would include our primary poetic experience), in which all thinking begins, to a transcendental or questioning attitude: to be *in* the world and yet not *of* the world, to be *inside* and *outside* at once.

How do you see this double fidelity to the philosophical and poetic attitudes operating in your own work?

My work operates on the basis of two overriding impulses or passions. On the one hand, it strives for scientific rigour and form – a striving epitomized by my preoccupation with the mathematical logic of relations and the search for the principle of reason. On the other hand, I began to wonder if this search for rigour and reason might not ultimately lead to the sterile tautologies of a *mathesis universalis*: the pretentious claim to possess an absolutely certain Principle–Foundation through a synthesis of Aristotelian logic, Euclidean geometry and the Scholastic doctrine of Transcendentals. And this doubt provided a space for the emergence of a second fundamental passion – what I might call my 'poetic inclination'. This second poetic passion challenged the speculative claim to absolute identity or totality and revived an attentiveness to the vibrant multiplicity of the lifeworld. I suppose this poetic inclination can be witnessed, in its modernist guise, in Mallarmé's notion of 'dissemination'. I chose the terms 'metaphor' and 'metamorphosis' to express this reality of movement, alteration and diversification. And Derrida, Lyotard, Deleuze and Lévinas have developed their respective philosophies of 'difference', repudiating the principle of identity for either the subject or the object. It is my own conviction that the classical metaphysics of identity and the modernist poetics of difference need each other, for both correspond to fundamental impulses in human thinking. This is what I tried to express in *Etre, monde, imaginaire* when I analysed how the speculative principle of the *Logos* and the poetic principle of the *Mythos* are committed to each other in a creative conflict which unfolds in the free space of the *imaginaire*. This act of faith in the 'imaginary', in the open horizon of the possible where oppositions confront and recreate each other, is where my initial reflections on the *Esse-in* and the *Esse-ad* have led me.

I might summarize this dual allegiance of my work as follows. To consider philosophy as an exclusively critical or speculative movement is to condemn it to an endless contestation which can easily slip into the nihilism of a *reductio ad absurdum*. Philosophy must continually remind itself of its origins in the bedrock of real experience. Only when one has experienced the opaque profundity of existential or religious reality can one legitimately take one's critical distance in order to question or reflect upon it. Similarly, it is only when one has been immersed in the social lifeworld that one can begin to interrogate the ideological structures which regulate it. Philosophy always presupposes the ability to say: *this* is what a tree is, *this* is how authority works, *this* is what a tribunal consists of, etc. The speculative instance is inextricably dependent upon the concrete immediacy of the person's lived experience. It cannot afford to ignore the existential conditions which precede it. I have always been struck by Suarez's principle of identity, which states that 'every being has an essence which constitutes and determines it'. Philosophy begins with a commitment to the determining world and only in an ulterior, reflexive moment proceeds to 'objectify' or 'formalize'. Philosophy does not begin with Kant – though the 'critical' turn is a crucial stage in its development. I think we should be grateful to Marx for having turned idealism on its head and for making it more humble towards reality; only by being engaged to the living body of history can critical thinking avoid becoming a corpse of solipsistic introspection. It is because philosophy is both *critique* and *commitment* that it can distance itself from the world precisely in order to transform it.

This summary analysis of your philosophy reminds me of your theological interpretation of the ecumenical dialectic between Catholic, Protestant and Orthodox thinking in *La Foi et raison logique*.

In this work I tried to rethink ecumenism in terms of a group of metaphysical operations. In this schema, the Catholic tradition privileged the operation of transitivity and transformation, functioning as a process of historical realism bound to the preservation of Revelation in the temporal world. The Protestant Reform privileged the operation of a critical conversion (turning around) which returned to the fundamental origins of Christianity. And thirdly, the Orthodox church of oriental Christianity privileged the operation of 'manence' (*Esse-in*) or in-dwelling. I argued that all three movements – of historical transformation, critical return and spiritual dwelling – are essential to the Christian reality, ensuring that it remains transitive and intransitive, transcendent and immanent. The history of Christianity is the drama of this divergence and belonging-together of Catholicism, Protestantism and Orthodoxy as a fecund tension between complementary differences. I think that ecumenism is facile if it ignores the importance of this creative tension. It is only when one assumes the specificity of one's own religious tradition (in my case Catholic) that one can fully appreciate the *other* – the essential contribution which the other traditions make to one's own.

France produced a considerable number of 'Christian philosophers' in the first half of this century, including Marcel, Mounier, Maritain and Gilson. Would you consider yourself a Christian philosopher?

I am a Christian philosopher to the extent that the primary experience that fostered and coloured much of my philosophical thinking was, as I explained at the outset, specifically Christian in certain respects – particularly as it determined my reflections on the Passion and the Cross. Such Christian reflection frequently dovetailed with my preoccupation with Greek and neoplatonic thought. For example, my description of the Cross as the 'seed of non-being' (*german nihili*) bears an intimate correspondence to Proclus's notion of the *sperma meontos*. The neoplatonic attempts to critically radicalize the Platonic philosophy of Being (*On*) find common ground here with the theology of the Cross. If the theology of

Glory – with its splendid doctrine of the superabundance of grace – is divorced from the critical theology of the Cross, it can degenerate into triumphalism. Grace is not power but dispossession because it is given under the interrogative sign of the Cross. To the extent, therefore, that the theology of the Cross deeply affected my whole attitude to thought, I would be prepared to consider myself a 'Christian' philosopher. But I would insist that philosophy and theology are separate, if equally valid, disciplines of thought. Whereas the theologian can presuppose the Christian tradition as a series of Revealed doctrines, the philosopher – even the Christian philosopher – cannot. The theologian believes truth is given, the philosopher goes in search of it.

Select bibliography of Stanislas Breton

L'Esse 'in' et l'esse 'ad' dans la métaphysique de la relation, Rome, 1951.
La Passion du Christ et les philosophies, Eco, Teramo, 1954.
Conscience et intentionalité, Vitte, Paris-Lyon, 1956.
Approches phénoménologiques de l'idée d'être, Vitte, Paris-Lyon, 1959.
Situation de la philosophie contemporaine, Vitte, Paris-Lyon, 1959.
Essence et existence, P.U.F., Paris, 1962.
Le Problème de l'être spirituel dans la philosophie de N. Hartman, Vitte, Paris-Lyon, 1962.
Mystique de la Passion, Desclée, Tournai, 1962.
Saint Thomas d'Aquin, Seghers, Paris, 1965.
Philosophie et mathématiques chez Proclus, Beauchesne, Paris, 1969.
Du principe, coéd. Aubier, Cerf, Desclée, Delachaux, Paris, 1971.
La Foi et raison logique, Le Seuil, Paris, 1971.
Etre, monde, imaginaire, Le Seuil, Paris, 1976.
Théorie des idéologies, Desclée, Paris, 1976.
Spinoza, Théologie et politique, Desclée, Paris, 1977.

Jacques Derrida

Prefatory note

Born in Algeria in 1931 to Jewish parents, Jacques Derrida is considered by many to be one of the most innovatory thinkers working on the Continent today. Along with Lacan, Foucault, Barthes and Lévi-Strauss, Derrida was largely responsible for putting the controversial structuralist/post-structuralist debate on the intellectual map. His influence has been paramount not only in France, where he studied and has taught now for many years at *l'Ecole Normale Supérieure*, but also in the Anglo-American world, where he has lectured widely in humanities and philosophy departments, serving as Visiting Professor at both Johns Hopkins and Yale universities.

Most celebrated for his systematic and unremitting 'deconstruction' of Western metaphysics, Derrida hails originally from the phenomenological movement of Husserl, Heidegger and Lévinas; and it is within and around this particular philosophical framework, more than any other, that his thinking has evolved. Derrida's earliest works were *Edmund Husserl's 'Origin of Geometry': An Introduction* (1962), and a critical analysis of Husserl's theory of the sign entitled *Speech and Phenomena* (1967) – this latter work being, by his own admission, 'the one to which (he) feels most attached'. Already in these early texts, Derrida was working out his central notion of the irreducible structure of *differance* as it operates in human consciousness, temporality, history and above all in the fundamental and overriding activity of writing (l'*écriture*). By means of this concept of *differance* – a neologism meaning both to 'defer' and to 'differ' – Derrida proposed to show how the major metaphysical definitions of Being as some timeless self-identity or presence (e.g. *logos*, *ousia*, *telos* and so on), which dominated Western philosophy from Plato to the present day, could ultimately be 'deconstructed'. Such a deconstruction would show that in each instance differance *precedes* presence rather than the contrary (as has been presupposed by what Derrida terms the 'logocentric' tradition of Western thought).

In his more mature works, in particular *Of Grammatology* (1967), *Writing and Difference* (1967), *Dissemination* (1972) and *Margins of Philosophy* (1972), Derrida has applied his 'deconstructive' analysis to a wide variety of subjects – literary, scientific, linguistic and psychoanalytic, as well as strictly philosophical. Indeed, his most recent work, marked by the publication of *Glas* in 1974 and followed by *Truth in Painting* (1978) and *The Postcard* (1980), freely experiments with new modes of thinking and writing in an attempt to overcome the rigid traditional divide between aesthetic and philosophical discourse: a divide determined by the 'logocentrism' of Western metaphysics which sought to exile from the realm of pure reason (*logos*) all that did not conform to its centralizing logic of identity and non-contradiction.

By redirecting our attention to the shifting 'margins' and limits which determine such logocentric procedures of exclusion and division, Derrida contrives to dismantle our preconceived notions of *identity* and expose us to the challenge of hitherto suppressed or concealed 'otherness' – the *other* side of experience, which has been ignored in order to preserve the illusion of truth as a perfectly self-contained and self-sufficient presence. Thus, for example, we find Derrida questioning and subverting the traditional priorities of speech over writing, presence over absence, sameness over difference, timelessness over time and so on. His work of rigorous deconstruction poses, accordingly, a radical challenge to such hallowed logocentric notions as the Eternal Idea of Plato, the Self-Thinking-Thought of Aristotle or the *cogito* of Descartes. For Derrida, there is nothing that has been thought that cannot be rethought, nothing can be said that cannot be unsaid. Even deconstruction itself must be deconstructed.

The following dialogue took place in Paris in 1981.

Deconstruction and the other

> **Richard Kearney:** The most characteristic feature of your work has been its determination to 'deconstruct' the Western philosophy of presence. I think it would be very helpful if you could situate your programme of deconstruction in relation to the two major intellectual traditions of Western culture – the Hebraic and the Hellenic. You conclude your seminal essay on the Jewish philosopher, Emmanuel Lévinas, with the following quotation from James Joyce's *Ulysses*: 'GreekJew is JewGreek'. Do you agree with Lévinas that Judaism offers an alternative to the Greek metaphysics of presence? Or do you believe with Joyce that the Jewish and Greek cultures are fundamentally intertwined?

Jacques Derrida: While I consider it essential to think through this copulative synthesis of Greek and Jew, I consider my own thought, paradoxically, as neither Greek nor Jewish. I often feel that the questions I attempt to formulate on the outskirts of the Greek philosophical tradition have as their 'other' the model of the Jew, that is, the Jew-as-other. And yet the paradox is that I have never actually invoked the Jewish tradition in any 'rooted' or direct manner. Though I was born a Jew, I do not work or think within a living Jewish tradition. So that if there is a Judaic dimension to my thinking which may from time to time have spoken in or through me, this has never assumed the form of an explicit fidelity or debt to that culture. In short, the ultimate site (*lieu*) of my questioning discourse would be neither Hellenic nor Hebraic if such were possible. It would be a non-site beyond both the Jewish influence of my youth and the Greek philosophical heritage which I received during my academic education in the French universities.

> And yet you share a singular discourse with Lévinas – including notions of the 'other', the 'trace' and writing as 'difference', etc. – which might suggest a common Judaic heritage.

Undoubtedly, I was fascinated and attracted by the intellectual journey of Lévinas, but that was not because he was Jewish. It so happens that for Lévinas there is a discrete continuity between his philosophical discourse qua phenomenologist and his religious language qua exegete of the Talmud. But this continuity is not immediately evident. The Lévinas who most interested me at the outset was the philosopher working in phenomenology and posing the question of the 'other' to phenomenology; the Judaic dimension remained at that stage a discrete rather than a decisive reference.

You ask if Judaism offers an alternative to the Greek philosophy of 'presence'. First we must ascertain what exactly we mean by 'presence'. The French or English words are, of course, neither Greek nor Jewish. So that when we use the word we presuppose a vast history of translation which leads from the Greek terms *ousia* and *on* to the Latin *substantia*, *actus*, etc. and culminates in our modern term 'presence'. I have no knowledge of what this term means in Judaism.

So you would account yourself a philosopher above all else?

I'm not happy with the term 'philosopher'.

Surely you are a philosopher in that your deconstruction is directed primarily to philosophical ideas and texts?

It is true that 'deconstruction' has focused on philosophical texts. And I am of course a 'philosopher' in the institutional sense that I assume the responsibilities of a teacher of philosophy in an official philosophical institution – *l'Ecole Normale Supérieure*. But I am not sure that the 'site' of my work, reading philosophical texts and posing philosophical questions, is itself properly philosophical. Indeed, I have attempted more and more systematically to find a non-site, or a non-philosophical site, from which to question philosophy. But the search for a non-philosophical site does not bespeak an anti-philosophical attitude. My central question is: from what site or non-site (*non-lieu*) can philosophy as such appear to itself as other than itself, so that it can interrogate and reflect upon itself in an original manner? Such a non-site or alterity would be radically irreducible to philosophy. But the problem is that such a non-site cannot be defined or situated by means of philosophical language.

The philosophy of deconstruction would seem, therefore, to be a deconstruction of philosophy. Is your interest in painting, psychoanalysis and literature – particularly the literary texts of Jabes, Bataille, Blanchot, Artaud and

Mallarmé – not an attempt to establish this non-philosophical site of which you speak?

Certainly, but one must remember that even though these sites are non-philosophical they still belong to our Western culture and so are never totally free from the marks of philosophical language. In literature, for example, philosophical language is still present in some sense; but it produces and presents itself as alienated from itself, at a remove, at a distance. This distance provides the necessary free space from which to interrogate philosophy anew; and it was my preoccupation with literary texts which enabled me to discern the problematic of *writing* as one of the key factors in the deconstruction of metaphysics.

Accepting the fact that you are seeking a non-philosophical site, you would, I presume, still acknowledge important philosophical influences on your thought. How, for example, would you situate your strategy of deconstruction in respect to the phenomenological movement?

My philosophical formation owes much to the thought of Hegel, Husserl and Heidegger. Heidegger is probably the most constant influence, and particularly his project of 'overcoming' Greek metaphysics. Husserl, whom I studied in a more studious and painstaking fashion, taught me a certain methodical prudence and reserve, a rigorous technique of unravelling and formulating questions. But I never shared Husserl's pathos for, and commitment to, a phenomenology of presence. In fact, it was Husserl's method that helped me to suspect the very notion of presence and the fundamental role it has played in all philosophies. My relationship with Heidegger is much more enigmatic and extensive: here my interest was not just *methodological* but *existential*. The themes of Heidegger's questioning always struck me as necessary – especially the 'ontological difference', the reading of Platonism and the relationship between language and Being. My discovery of the genealogical and genetic critique of Nietszche and Freud also helped me to take the step beyond phenomenology towards a more radical, 'non-philosophical' questioning, while never renouncing the discipline and methodological rigour of phenomenology.

Although you share Heidegger's task of 'overcoming' or 'deconstructing' Western metaphysics, you would not, presumably, share his hope to rediscover the 'original names' by means of which Being could be thought and said?

I think that there is still in Heidegger, linked up with other things, a nostalgic desire to recover the proper name, the unique name of Being. To be fair, however, one can find several passages in which Heidegger is self-critical and renounces his nostalgia: his practice of cancelling and erasing the term in his later texts is an example of such a critique. Heidegger's texts are still before us; they harbour a future of meaning which will ensure that they are read and reread for centuries. But while I owe a considerable debt to Heidegger's 'path of thought' (*chemin de pensée*), we differ in our employment of language, in our understanding of language. I write in another language – and I do not simply mean in French rather than in German – even though this 'otherness' cannot be explained in terms of philosophy itself. The difference resides outside of philosophy, in the non-philosophical site of language; it is what makes the poets and writers that interest me (Mallarmé, Blanchot, etc.) totally different from those that interest Heidegger (Hölderlin and Rilke). In this sense my profound rapport with Heidegger is also and at the same time a non-rapport.

Yes, I can see that your understanding of language as 'differance' and 'dissemination' is quite removed from Heidegger's notion of language as the 'house of Being', that which 'recalls and recollects' and 'names the Holy'. In addition, while Heidegger is still prepared to use such philosophical concepts as *Being* and *existence* to express his thought, you have made it clear that the operative terms in your language – e.g. deconstruction, differance, dissemination, trace and so on – are basically 'non-concepts', 'undecidables'. What exactly do you mean by 'non-concepts' and what role do they play in your attempt to deconstruct metaphysics?

I will try to reconstitute the argument by means of which I advanced the notion of a non-concept. First, it doesn't have the logical generality which a philosophical concept claims to have in its supposed independence from ordinary or literary language. The notion of 'differance', for example, is a non-concept in that it cannot be defined in terms of oppositional predicates; it is neither *this* nor *that*; but rather this *and* that (e.g. the act of differing and of deferring) without being reducible to a dialectical logic either. And yet the term 'differance' emerges and develops as a determination of language from which it is inseparable. Hence the difficulty of translating the term. There is no conceptual realm beyond language which would allow the term to have a univocal semantic content over and above its inscription in language. Because it remains a trace of language it remains non-conceptual. And because it has no oppositional or predicative generality, which would identify it as *this* rather than *that*, the term 'differance' cannot be defined within a system of logic – Aristotelian or dialectical – that is, within the logocentric system of philosophy.

> But can we go beyond or deconstruct the logocentric system of metaphysics without employing the terminology of metaphysics? Is it not only *from the inside* that we can undo metaphysics by means of stratagems and strategies which expose the ambiguities and contradictions of the logocentric system of presence? Does that not mean that we are condemned to metaphysics even while attempting to deconstruct its pretensions?

In a certain sense it is true to say that 'deconstruction' is still *in* metaphysics. But we must remember that if we are indeed *inside* metaphysics, we are not inside it as we might be *inside* a box or a milieu. We are still *in* metaphysics in the special sense that we are *in* a determinate language. Consequently, the idea that we might be able to get outside of metaphysics has always struck me as naive. So that when I refer to the 'closure' (*clôture*) of metaphysics, I insist that it is not a question of considering metaphysics as a circle with a limit or simple boundary. The notion of the limit and boundary (*bord*) of metaphysics is itself highly problematic. My reflections on this problematic have always attempted to show that the limit or end of metaphysics is not linear or circular in any indivisible sense. And as soon as we acknowledge that the limit-boundary of metaphysics is divisible, the logical rapport between inside and outside is no longer simple. Accordingly, we cannot really say that we are 'locked into' or 'condemned to' metaphysics, for we are, strictly speaking, neither inside nor outside. In brief, the whole rapport between the inside and the outside of metaphysics is inseparable from the question of the finitude and reserve of metaphysics as language. But the idea of the finitude and exhaustion (*épuisement*) of metaphysics does not mean that we are incarcerated in it as prisoners or victims of some unhappy fatality. It is simply that our belonging to, and inherence in, the language of metaphysics is something that can only be rigorously and adequately thought about from *another* topos or space where our problematic rapport with the boundary of metaphysics can be seen in a more radical light. Hence my attempts to discover the non-place or *non-lieu* which would be the 'other' of philosophy. This is the task of deconstruction.

> Can literary and poetic language provide this *non-lieu* or *u-topos*?

I think so; but when I speak of literature it is not with a capital L; it is rather an allusion to certain movements which have worked around the limits of our logical concepts, certain texts which make the limits of our language tremble, exposing them as divisible and questionable. This is what the works of Blanchot, Bataille or Beckett are particularly sensitive to.

> What does this whole problematic of the closure of Western 'logocentric' philosophy and of the limits of our language tell us about the modern age in which we live? Is there a rapport between deconstruction and 'modernity' in so far as the latter bespeaks a crisis of scientific foundations and of values in general, a crisis occasioned by the discovery that the absolute origin that the Western tradition claimed to have identified in the 'logos' is merely the trace of an absence, a nothingness?

I have never been very happy with the term 'modernity'. Of course, I feel that what is happening in the world today is something unique and singular. As soon, however, as we give it the label of 'modernity', we inscribe it in a certain historical system of evolution or progress (a notion derived from Enlightenment rationalism) which tends to blind us to the fact that what confronts us today is *also* something ancient and hidden in history. I believe that what 'happens' in our contemporary world and strikes us as particularly new has in fact an essential connection with something extremely old which has been covered over (*archi-dissimulé*). So that the new is not so much that which occurs for the first time but that 'very ancient' dimension which recurs in the 'very modern'; and which indeed has been signified repetitively throughout our historical tradition, in Greece and in Rome, in Plato and in

Descartes and in Kant, etc. No matter how novel or unprecedented a modern meaning may appear, it is never exclusively *modernist* but is also and at the same time a phenomenon of *repetition*. And yet the relationship between the ancient and the modern is not simply that of the implicit and the explicit. We must avoid the temptation of supposing that what occurs today somehow pre-existed in a latent form, merely waiting to be unfolded or explicated. Such thinking also conceives history as an evolutionary development and excludes the crucial notions of rupture and mutation in history. My own conviction is that we must maintain two contradictory affirmations at the same time. On the one hand we affirm the existence of ruptures in history, and on the other we affirm that these ruptures produce gaps or faults (*failles*) in which the most hidden and forgotten archives can emerge and constantly recur and work through history. One must surmount the categorical oppositions of philosophical logic out of fidelity to these conflicting positions of historical discontinuity (rupture) and continuity (repetition), which are neither a pure break with the past nor a pure unfolding or explication of it.

> How do you explain the way in which philosophy has altered and changed from one historical epoch to the next? How do you explain, for example, the difference between Plato's thought and your own?

The difference between our modes of thought does not mean that I or other 'modern' thinkers have gone beyond Plato, in the sense of having succeeding in exhausting all that is contained in his texts. Here I return to what I was describing as the 'future' of a Heideggerian text. I believe that all of the great philosophical texts – of Plato, Parmenides, Hegel or Heidegger, for example – are still *before* us. The future of the great philosophies remains obscure and enigmatic, still to be disclosed. Up to now, we have merely scratched the surface. This opaque and inexhaustible residue of philosophical texts, which I call their 'future', is more predominant in Greek and German philosophy than in French. I have a profound respect for the great French thinkers, but I have always had the impression that a certain kind of rigorous analysis could render their texts accessible and exhaustible. Before a Platonic or Heideggerian text, by contrast, I feel that I am confronting an abyss, a bottomless pit in which I could lose myself. No matter how rigorous an analysis

I bring to bear on such texts, I am always left with the impression that there is something *more* to be thought.

> What exactly is the inexhaustible richness which these great texts possess and which continues to fascinate us throughout the centuries?

The temptation here is to offer a quick and simple response. But having taught philosophy for over twenty years, I must honestly say that now, less than ever, do I know what philosophy is. My knowledge of what it is that constitutes the essence of philosophy is at zero degree. All I know is that a Platonic or Heideggerian text always returns us to the beginning, enables us to *begin* to ask philosophical questions, including the question: what is philosophy?

> But surely it must be possible to say *what* philosophy is by way of distinguishing it from other scientific disciplines such as economics, sociology, the natural sciences, or even literature? Why learn philosophy at all, in schools, universities or in the privacy of one's study, if it is impossible to say what it is or what function it serves? If deconstruction prevents us from asserting or stating or identifying anything, then surely one ends up, not with 'differance', but with indifference, where nothing is anything, and everything is everything else?

It is as impossible to say what philosophy *is not* as it is to say what it *is*. In all the other disciplines you mention, there is philosophy. To say to oneself that one is going to study something that is *not* philosophy is to deceive oneself. It is not difficult to show that in political economy, for example, there is a philosophical discourse in operation. And the same applies to mathematics and the other sciences. Philosophy, as logocentrism, is present in every scientific discipline and the only justification for transforming philosophy into a specialized discipline is the necessity to render explicit and thematic the philosophical subtext in every discourse. The principal function which the teaching of philosophy serves is to enable people to become 'conscious', to become aware of what exactly they are saying, what kind of discourse they are engaged in when they do mathematics, physics, political economy, and so on. There is no system of teaching or transmitting knowledge which can retain its coherence or integrity without, at one moment or another, interrogating itself philosophically, that is, without acknowledging its subtextual premisses; and this may even include an interrogation of unspoken political interests or traditional values. From such an interrogation each society draws its own conclusions about the worth of philosophy.

How, for example, can political economy interrogate itself philosophically?

First, all of the major concepts which constitute the discourse of economics are philosophical, and particularly such concepts as 'property', 'work' or 'value'. These are all 'philosophemes', concepts inaugurated by a philosophical discourse which usually go back to Greece or Rome, and kept in operation by means of this discourse, which refers back at first, as does philosophy itself, to the 'natural languages' of Greece and Rome. Consequently, the economic discourse is founded on a logocentric philosophical discourse and remains inseparable from it. The 'autonomy' which economists might subsequently like to confer on their discipline can never succeed in masking its philosophical derivation. Science is never purely objective, nor is it merely reducible to an instrumental and utilitarian model of explanation. Philosophy can teach science that it is ultimately an element of language, that the limits of its formalization reveal its belonging to a language in which it continues to operate despite its attempts to justify itself as an exclusively 'objective' or 'instrumental' discourse.

Is the logocentric character of science a singularly European phenomenon?

Logocentrism, in its developed philosophical sense, is inextricably linked to the Greek and European tradition. As I have attempted to demonstrate elsewhere in some detail, logocentric philosophy is a specifically Western response to a much larger necessity which also occurs in the Far East and other cultures, that is, the phonocentric necessity: the privilege of the voice over writing. The priority of spoken language over written or silent language stems from the fact that when words are spoken the speaker and the listener are supposed to be simultaneously present to one another; they are supposed to be the same, pure unmediated presence. This ideal of perfect self-presence, of the immediate possession of meaning, is what is expressed by the phonocentric necessity. Writing, on the other hand, is considered subversive in so far as it creates a spatial and temporal distance between the author and audience; writing presupposes the absence of the author and so we can never be sure exactly what is meant by a written text; it can have many different meanings as opposed to a single unifying one. But this phonocentric necessity did not develop into a systematic logocentric metaphysics in any non-European culture. Logocentrism is a uniquely European phenomenon.

> Does this mean that other cultures do not require deconstruction?

Every culture and society requires an internal critique or deconstruction as an essential part of its development. *A priori*, we can presume that non-European cultures operate some sort of auto-critique of their own linguistic concepts and foundational institutions. Every culture needs an element of self-interrogation and of distance from itself, if it is to transform itself. No culture is closed in on itself, expecially in our own times when the impact of European civilization is so all-pervasive. Similarly, what we call the deconstruction of our own Western culture is aided and abetted by the fact that Europe has always registered the impact of heterogeneous, non-European influences. Because it has always been thus exposed to, and shadowed by, its 'other', it has been compelled to question itself. Every culture is haunted by its other.

> Did the arrival of Judeo-Christianity represent such a radicalizing 'alterity' for the Graeco-Roman civilization? Did it challenge the homogeneity of the Western metaphysics of presence?

I'd be wary of talking about Judeo-Christianity with a capital J and C. Judeo-Christianity is an extremely complex entity which, in large part, only constituted itself qua Judeo-Christianity by its assimilation into the schemas of Greek philosophy. Hence what we know as Christian and Jewish theology today is a cultural ensemble which has already been largely 'Hellenized'.

> But did not Judaism and Christianity represent a heterogeneity, an 'otherness' before they were assimilated into Greek culture?

Of course. And one can argue that these original, heterogeneous elements of Judaism and Christianity were never completely eradicated by Western metaphysics. They perdure throughout the centuries, threatening and unsettling the assured 'identities' of Western philosophy. So that the surreptitious deconstruction of the Greek *Logos* is at work from the very origin of our Western culture. Already, the translation of Greek concepts into other languages – Latin, Arabic, German, French, English, etc. – or indeed the translation of Hebraic or Arabic ideas and structures into metaphysical terms, produces 'fissures' in the presumed 'solidity' of Greek philosophy by introducing alien and conflicting elements.

> The logocentrism of Greek metaphysics will always be haunted, therefore, by the 'absolutely other' to the extent that the *Logos* can never englobe everything. There is always something which escapes, something different, other and opaque which refuses to be totalized into a homogeneous identity.

Just so – and this 'otherness' is not necessarily something which comes to Greek philosophy from the 'outside', that is, from the non-Hellenic world. From the very beginnings of Greek philosophy the self-identity of the *Logos* is already fissured and divided. I think one can discern signs of such fissures of 'differance' in every great philosopher: the 'Good beyond Being' (*epekeina tes ousias*) of Plato's *Republic*, for example, or the confrontation with the 'Stranger' in *The Sophist* are already traces of an alterity which refuses to be totally domesticated. Moreover, the rapport of self-identity is itself always a rapport of violence with the other; so that the notions of property, appropriation and self-presence, so central to logocentric metaphysics, are essentially dependent on an oppositional relation with otherness. In this sense, identity *presupposes* alterity.

> If deconstruction is a way of challenging the logocentric pretensions of Western philosophy, and by implication of the sciences it has founded, can it ever surmount its role of iconoclastic negation and become a form of affirmation? Can your search for a non-site or *u-topos*, other than the *topos* of Western metaphysics, also be construed as a prophetic utopianism?

I will take the terms 'affirmation' and 'prophetic utopianism' separately. Deconstruction certainly entails a moment of affirmation. Indeed, I cannot conceive of a radical critique which would not be ultimately motivated by some sort of affirmation, acknowledged or not. Deconstruction always presupposes affirmation, as I have frequently attempted to point out, sometimes employing a Nietzschean terminology. I do not mean that the deconstructing *subject* or *self* affirms. I mean that deconstruction is, in itself, a positive response to an alterity which necessarily calls, summons or motivates it. Deconstruction is therefore vocation – a response to a call. The other, as the other than self, the other that opposes self-identity, is not something that can be detected and disclosed within a philosophical space and with the aid of a philosophical lamp. The other precedes philosophy and necessarily invokes and provokes the subject before any genuine questioning can begin. It is in this rapport with the other that affirmation expresses itself.

As to the question of prophecy, this is a much more obscure area for me. There are certainly prophetic effects (*effets*); but the language of prophecy alters continually. Today the prophets no longer speak with the same accents or scenography as the prophets in the Bible.

> Lévinas has suggested that the contemporary deconstruction of philosophy and the sciences is symptomatic of a fundamental crisis of Western culture, which he chooses to interpret as a prophetic and ethical cry. Would you agree?

Certainly prophets always flourish in times of socio-historical or philosophical crisis. Bad times for philosophy are good times for prophecy. Accordingly, when deconstructive themes begin to dominate the scene, as they do today, one is sure to find a proliferation of prophecies. And this proliferation is precisely a reason why we should be all the more wary and prudent, all the more discriminating.

> But here we have the whole problem of a criterion of evaluation. According to what criterion does one discriminate between prophecies? Is this not a problem for you since you reject the idea of a transcendental *telos* or *eschaton* which could provide the critical subject with an objective or absolute yardstick of value?

It is true that I interrogate the idea of an *eschaton* or *telos* in the absolute formulations of classical philosophy. But that does not mean I dismiss all forms of Messianic or prophetic eschatology. I think that all genuine questioning is summoned by a certain type of eschatology, though it is impossible to define this eschatology in philosophical terms. The search for objective or absolute criteria is, to be sure, an essentially philosophical gesture. Prophecy differs from philosophy in so far as it dispenses with such criteria. The prophetic word is its own criterion and refuses to submit to an external tribunal which would judge or evaluate it in an objective and neutral fashion. The prophetic word reveals its own eschatology and finds its index of truthfulness in its own inspiration and not in some transcendental or philosophical criteriology.

Do you feel that your own work is prophetic in its attempt to deconstruct philosophy and philosophical criteria?

Unfortunately, I do not feel inspired by any sort of hope which would permit me to presume that my work of deconstruction has a prophetic function. But I concede that the style of my questioning as an exodus and dissemination in the desert might produce certain prophetic resonances. It is possible to see deconstruction as being produced in a space where the prophets are not far away. But the prophetic resonances of my questioning reside at the level of a certain rhetorical discourse which is also shared by several other contemporary thinkers. The fact that I declare it 'unfortunate' that I do not personally feel inspired may be a signal that deep down I still hope. It means that I am in fact still looking for something. So perhaps it is no mere accident of rhetoric that the search itself, the search without hope for hope, assumes a certain prophetic *allure*. Perhaps my search is a twentieth century brand of prophecy? But it is difficult for me to believe it.

Can the theoretical radicality of deconstruction be translated into a radical political praxis?

This is a particularly difficult question. I must confess that I have never succeeded in directly relating deconstruction to existing political codes and programmes. I have of course had occasion to take a specific political stand in certain codable situations, for example, in relation to the French university institution. But the available codes for taking such a political stance are not at all adequate to the radicality of deconstruction. And the absence of an adequate political code to translate or incorporate the radical implications of deconstruction has given many the impression that deconstruction is opposed to politics, or is at best apolitical. But this impression only prevails because all of our political codes and terminologies still remain fundamentally metaphysical, regardless of whether they originate from the right or the left.

> In *The Revolution of the Word*, Colin McCabe employed your notions of deconstruction and dissemination to show how James Joyce recognized and revealed the inner workings of language as a refusal of identity, as a process of 'differance' irreducible to all of our logocentric concepts and codes. In *Ulysses* this process of 'differance' is epitomized by Bloom, the vagrant or nomad who obviates and subverts the available codes of identity – religious, political or national. And yet, McCabe argues, the Joycean refutation of all dogmatic or totalizing forms of identity is itself a political stance – an anti-totalitarian or anarchic stance.

This is the politics of exodus, of the emigré. As such, it can of course serve as a political ferment or anxiety, a subversion of fixed assumptions and a privileging of disorder.

> But does the politics of the emigré necessarily imply inaction and non-commitment?

Not at all. But the difficulty is to gesture in opposite directions at the same time: on the one hand to preserve a distance and suspicion with regard to the official political codes governing reality; on the other, to intervene here and now in a practical and *engagé* manner whenever the necessity arises. This position of dual allegiance, in which I personally find myself, is one of perpetual uneasiness. I try where I can to act politically while recognizing that such action remains incommensurate with my intellectual project of deconstruction.

> Could one describe the political equivalent of deconstruction as a disposition, as opposed to a position, of responsible anarchy?

If I had to describe my political disposition I would probably employ a formula of that kind while stressing, of course, the interminable obligation to work out and to deconstruct these two terms – 'responsible' and 'anarchy'. If taken as assured certainties in themselves, such terms can also become reified and unthinking dogmas. But I also try to re-evaluate the indispensable notion of 'responsibility'.

> I would now like to turn to another theme in your work: the deconstructive role of the 'feminine'. If the logocentric domination of Western culture also expresses itself as a 'phallogocentrism', is there a sense in which the modern movement to liberate women represents a deconstructive gesture? Is this something which Nietzsche curiously recognized when he spoke of 'truth becoming woman'; or Joyce when he celebrated the 'woman's reason' of Molly Bloom in *Ulysses* and Anna Livia Plurabelle in *Finnegans Wake*? Is the contemporary liberation of woman's reason and truth not an unveiling of the hitherto repressed resources of a non-logocentric *topos*?

While I would hesitate to use such terms as 'liberation' or 'unveiling', I think there can be little doubt that we are presently witnessing a radical mutation of our understanding of sexual difference. The discourses of Nietzsche, Joyce and the women's movement which you have identified epitomize a profound and unprecedented transformation of the man–woman relationship. The deconstruction of phallogocentrism is carried by this transformation, as are also the rise of psychoanalysis and the modernist movement in literature. But we cannot objectify or thematize this mutation even though it is bringing about such a radical change in our understanding of the world that a return to the former logocentric philosophies of mastery, possession, totalization or certitude may soon be unthinkable. The philosphical and literary discoveries of the 'feminine' which you mention – and even the political and legal recognition of the status of women – are all symptoms of a deeper mutation in our search for meaning which deconstruction attempts to register.

> Do you think then that this mutation can be seen and evaluated in terms of an historical progress towards the 'good', towards a 'better' society?

This mutation is certainly experienced as 'better' in so far as it is what is desired by those who practically dispose of the greatest 'force' in society. One could describe the transformation effected by the feminine as 'good' without positing it as an *a priori* goal or telos. I hesitate to speak of 'liberation' in this context, because I don't believe that women are 'liberated', any more than men are. They are, of course, no longer 'enslaved' in many of the old socio-political respects, but even in the new situation woman will not ultimately be any freer than man. One needs another language, besides that of political liberation, to characterize the enormous deconstructive import of the feminine as an uprooting of our phallogocentric culture. I prefer to speak of this mutation of the feminine as a 'movement' rather than as an historical or political 'progress'. I always hesitate to talk of historical progress.

What is the relationship between deconstruction and your use of poetic language, particularly in *Glas*? Do you consider *Glas* to be a work of philosophy or of poetry?

It is neither philosophy nor poetry. It is in fact a reciprocal contamination of the one by the other, from which neither can emerge intact. This notion of contamination is, however, inadequate, for it is not simply a question of rendering both philosophy and poetry *impure*. One is trying to reach an additional or alternative dimension beyond philosophy and literature. In my project, philosophy and literature are two poles of an opposition and one cannot isolate one from the other or privilege one over the other. I consider that the limits of philosophy are also those of literature. In *Glas*, consequently, I try to compose a *writing* which would traverse, as rigorously as possible, both the philosophical and literary elements without being definable as either. Hence in *Glas* one finds classical philosophical analysis being juxtaposed with quasi-literary passages, each challenging, perverting and exposing the impurities and contradictions in their neighbour; and at some point the philosophical and literary trajectories cross each other and give rise to something else, some *other* site.

Is there not a sense in which philosophy for you is a form of literature? You have, for example, described metaphysics as a 'white mythology', that is, a sort of palimpsest of metaphors (*eidos, telos, ousia*) and myths (of return, homecoming, transcendence towards the light, etc.), which are covered over and forgotten as soon as philosophical 'concepts' are construed as pure and univocal abstractions, as totalizing universals devoid of myth and metaphor.

I have always tried to expose the way in which philosophy is literary, not so much because it is *metaphor* but because it is *catachresis*. The term metaphor generally implies a relation to an original 'property' of meaning, a 'proper' sense to which it indirectly or equivocally refers, whereas catachresis is a violent production of meaning, an abuse which refers to no anterior or proper norm. The founding concepts of metaphysics – *logos, eidos, theoria*, etc. – are instances of *catachresis* rather than metaphors as I attempted to demonstrate in 'White Mythology' (*Marges de la philosophie*). In a work such as *Glas*, or other recent ones like it, I am trying to produce new forms of catachresis, another kind of writing, a violent writing which stakes out the faults (*failles*) and deviations of language; so that the text produces a language of its own, in itself, which while continuing to work through tradition emerges at a given moment as a *monster*, a monstrous mutation without tradition or normative precedent.

What then of the question of language as reference? Can language as mutation or violence or monstrosity refer to anything other than itself?

There have been several misinterpretations of what I and other deconstructionists are trying to do. It is totally false to suggest that deconstruction is a suspension of reference. Deconstruction is always deeply concerned with the 'other' of language. I never cease to be surprised by critics who see my work as a declaration that there is nothing beyond language, that we are imprisoned in language; it is, in fact, saying the exact opposite. The critique of logocentrism is above all else the search for the 'other' and the 'other of language'. Every week I receive critical commentaries and studies on deconstruction which operate on the assumption that what they call 'post-structuralism' amounts to saying that there is nothing beyond language, that we are submerged in words – and other stupidities of that sort. Certainly, deconstruction tries to show that the question of reference is much more complex and problematic than traditional theories supposed. It even asks whether our term 'reference' is entirely adequate for designating the 'other'. The other, which is beyond language and which summons language, is perhaps not a 'referent' in the normal sense which linguists have attached to this term. But to distance oneself thus from the habitual structure of reference, to challenge or complicate our common assumptions about it, does not amount to saying that there is *nothing* beyond language.

> This could also be seen as a reply to those critics who maintain that deconstruction is a strategy of nihilism, an orgy of non-sense, a relapse into the free play of the arbitrary.

I regret that I have been misinterpreted in this way, particularly in the United States, but also in France. People who wish to avoid questioning and discussion present deconstruction as a sort of gratuitous chess game with a combination of signs (*combinatoire de signifiants*), closed up in language as in a cave. This misinterpretation is not just a simplification; it is symptomatic of certain political and institutional interests – interests which must also be deconstructed in their turn. I totally refuse the label of nihilism which has been ascribed to me and my American colleagues. Deconstruction is not an enclosure in nothingness, but an openness towards the other.

> Can deconstruction serve as a method of literary criticism which might contribute something positive to our appreciation of literature?

I am not sure that deconstruction can function as a literary *method* as such. I am wary of the idea of methods of reading. The laws of reading are determined by the particular text that is being read. This does not mean that we should simply abandon ourselves to the text, or represent and repeat it in a purely passive manner. It means that we must remain faithful, even if it implies a certain violence, to the injunctions of the text. These injunctions will differ from one text to the next so that one cannot prescribe one general method of reading. In this sense deconstruction is not a method. Nor do I feel that the principle function of deconstruction is to contribute something to literature. It does, of course, contribute to our epistemological appreciation of texts by exposing the philosophical and theoretical presuppositions that are at work in every critical methodology, be it Formalism, New Criticism, Socialist Realism or a historical critique. Deconstruction asks *why* we read a literary text in this particular manner rather than another. It shows, for example, that New Criticism is not *the* way of reading texts, however enshrined it may be in certain university institutions, but only one way among others. Thus deconstruction can also serve to question the presumption of certain university and cultural institutions to act as the sole or privileged guardians and transmitters of meaning. In short, deconstruction not only teaches us to read literature more thoroughly by attending to it *as language*, as the production of meaning through *differance* and dissemination, through a complex play of signifying traces; it also enables us to interrogate the covert philosophical and political presuppositions of institutionalized critical methods which generally govern our reading of a text. There is in deconstruction something which challenges every teaching institution. It is not a question of calling for the destruction of such institutions, but rather of making us aware of what we are in fact doing when we subscribe to this or that institutional way of reading literature. Nor must we forget that deconstruction is itself a form of literature, a literary text to be read like other texts, an interpretation open to several other interpretations. Accordingly, one can say that deconstruction is at once extremely *modest* and extremely *ambitious*. It is ambitious in that it puts itself on a par with literary texts, and modest in that it admits that it is only one textual interpretation among others, written in a language which has no centralizing power of mastery or domination, no privileged meta-language over and above the language of literature.

And what would you say to those critics who accuse you of annihilating the very idea of the human subject in your determination to dispense with all centralizing agencies of meaning, all 'centrisms'?

They need not worry. I have never said that the subject should be dispensed with. Only that it should be deconstructed. To deconstruct the subject does not mean to deny its existence. There are subjects, 'operations' or 'effects' (*effets*) of subjectivity. This is an incontrovertible fact. To acknowledge this does not mean, however, that the subject is what it *says* it is. The subject is not some meta-linguistic substance or identity, some pure *cogito* of self-presence; it is always inscribed in language. My work does not, therefore, destroy the subject; it simply tries to resituate it.

But can deconstruction, as the disclosure of language as *differance*, contribute to the *pleasure* of reading, to our appreciation of the living *texture* of a literary text? Or is it only an intellectual strategy of detection, of exposing our presuppositions and disabusing us of our habitual illusions about reading?

Deconstruction gives pleasure in that it gives desire. To deconstruct a text is to disclose how it functions as desire, as a search for presence and fulfilment which is interminably deferred. One cannot read without opening oneself to the desire of language, to the search for that which remains absent and other than oneself. Without a certain love of the text, no reading would be possible. In every reading there is a *corps-à-corps* between reader and text, an incorporation of the reader's desire into the desire of the text. Here is pleasure, the very opposite of that arid intellectualism of which deconstruction has so often been accused.

Select bibliography of Jacques Derrida

Introduction à l'origine de la géométrie de Husserl, P.U.F., Paris, 1962; English translation J.P. Leavey Jr., *Edmund Husserl's 'Origin of Geometry': An Introduction*, Humanities Press, New Jersey, 1978.

L'Ecriture et la différence, Editions du Seuil, Paris, 1967; English translation A. Bass, *Writing and Difference*, University of Chicago Press, Chicago, 1978.

La Voix et le phénomène, P.U.F., Paris, 1967; English translation D. Allison, *Speech and Phenomena and other Essays in Husserl's Theory of Signs*, Northwestern University Press, Evanston, 1973.

De la grammatologie, Editions de Minuit, Paris, 1967; English translation G. Spivak, *Of Grammatology*, Johns Hopkins University Press, Baltimore and London, 1977.

La Dissémination, Editions du Seuil, Paris, 1972; English translation B. Johnson, *Dissemination*, Athlone Press, London, 1981.

Marges de la philosophie, Editions de Minuit, Paris, 1972; English translation A. Bass, University of Chicago Press, Chicago (forthcoming).

Positions, Editions de Minuit, Paris, 1972; English translation A. Bass, *Positions*, University of Chicago Press, Chicago, 1977.

L'Archéologie du frivole, Editions Galilée, Paris, 1973.

Glas, Editions Galilée, Paris, 1974.

Eperons. Les Styles de Nietzsche, Venice, 1976; English translation, *Spurs: Nietzsche Styles*, University of Chicago Press, Chicago, 1979.

La Vérité en peinture, Flammarion, Paris, 1978.

La Carte postale: de Socrate à Freud et au-delà, Flammarion, Paris, 1980; English translation A. Bass, *The Postcard: From Socrates to Freud and Beyond*, University of Chicago Press, Chicago (forthcoming).

Appendix

'For speculation turns not to itself
Till it hath travell'd, and is mirror'd there
Where it may see itself.'
Shakespeare, *Troilus and Cressida*, Act III, Scene III

A note on the hermeneutics of dialogue

The model of modern hermeneutics is perhaps best outlined by Heidegger in *Being and Time* when he argues that all scientific and philosophical *reflection* is preceded by a *prereflective* lived experience of our being-in-the-world: a being which expresses itself primordially in the existential category of 'discourse' (*Rede*). The logical order of timeless, clear and distinct ideas can therefore no longer be considered as primary; it presupposes a 'saying' (*Sprechen*) which involves one in a historical community of speakers. Consequently our being-in-the-woirld (qua *Dasein*) is revealed historically in and through language as a dialogical being-in-the-world-with-others (qua *Mitsein*).

Hölderlin states this primacy of dialogical saying in the following celebrated lines of an unfinished poem:

> Viel hat erfahren der Mensch . . .
> Seit ein Gespräch wir sind
> Und hören können voneinander
>
> (Much has man experienced . . .
> Since we are a dialogue
> And can listen to one another)

Heidegger offers an illuminating gloss on these lines in a passage from his *Commentaries on Hölderlin's Poetry*:

> The being of man is grounded in language; but this really happens only in dialogue (i.e. in speaking and hearing) . . . From the time man places himself in the presence of something enduring, only from then can he expose himself to the changeable, the coming and the going. . . . We

> have been a dialogue since the time that 'time is'. Since time has arisen and has been brought to standing, since then we have been historical. Both – being-in-dialogue and being-historical – are equally old, belong together, and are the same.[1]

Inheriting and developing this hermeneutic model, Gadamer and Ricoeur point out that human consciousness can never know itself in terms of an intuitive immediacy (as Descartes or the early Husserl believed): consciousness must undergo a hermeneutic detour in which it comes to know itself through the mediation of signs, symbols and texts. In other words, consciousness cannot *intuit* (*anschauen*) its meaning in and from itself, but must *interpret* (*hermeneuein*) itself by entering into dialogue with the texts of a historical community or common tradition to which it belongs (*zuhören*).

History, as the communal becoming and preservation of meaning, is a dialogue precisely because man cannot live by his own subjectivity alone. I derive my meaning through my relationship with the other (be it the individual, communal or ontological other). To say accordingly that truth is dialogue does not necessitate a return to the Romantic hermeneutic model, advanced by Schleiermacher and others, which construes dialogue in terms of a perfect inter-subjective correspondence between one speaker and another. On the contrary, the dialogical model of hermeneutics variously developed by Heidegger, Gadamar, Ricoeur and Lévinas insists that meaning always originates in some source *other* than the intuitive immediacies of subjectivity or even intersubjectivity. Meaning always remains irreducible to the immediacy of the speaking subjects, coexisting in a homogeneous time or space. The Romantic model of dialogue as a mutually intuitive correspondence between two human presences is no more than one possible and derived expression of the more fundamental model of a 'hermeneutic circle' in which meaning always remains *prior* to the contemporaneous co-presence of subjectivities. We do not and cannot miraculously create meaning out of ourselves. We inherit meaning from others who have thought, spoken or written before us. And wherever possible, we *recreate* this meaning, according to our own projects and interpretations. But we are always obliged to listen to (*hören*) what has already been spoken, in other times and places, before we can in turn speak for ourselves in the here and now.

This is a crucial distinction, particularly as it pertains to the dialogue contained in this book. We are concerned here with 'dialogue' in the sense of a spoken communication between two subjects recorded and inscribed as a written text. This passage from *speaking* to *writing* is vitally important. For when a discourse passes from speaking to writing, the entire set of co-ordinates in the dialogue – *subject, word* and *world* – undergo a significant change. What is involved is more than a mere external fixation of the spoken words which would preserve them from temporal obliteration. The inscription of a dialogue in writing grants the text an autonomy with respect to the subjective intentions of the authors. Otherwise stated, textual meaning, even in the case of a written conversation, can no longer be deemed to coincide completely with the original intentions of the speakers. While it presupposes and expresses these intentions, it also manages to *exceed* them. Once committed to writing, the meaning of the speakers is distanced or 'distanciated' in some fundamental respect. And in the process, the text transcends the finite intentional horizons of the two interlocutors and opens up new horizons of meaning: the possible worlds of the text which lend themselves to the multiplicity of the reader's own interpretations. We thus discover that the original overlapping of the two speakers' horizons (*Horizontverschmelzung*),[2] is subjected to the additional overlapping of these same horizons with the reader's own infinitely extending horizons. Put in another way, the speakers' original intentions are doubly distanced in the hermeneutic process of textual inscription and reading.

The written dialogue is in itself an open invitation to the reader to fill in the gaps between the original speakers' words. It summons the reader to re-create and reinterpret the authors' original meanings according to his or her own hermeneutic and experiential presuppositions. In this sense, we might say that once the reader has entered the dialogue, it becomes a dialogue that never ends. Laurence Sterne expressed this point succinctly, albeit mischievously, when he addressed his readers in *Tristram Shandy*: 'Writing when properly managed . . . is but a different name for conversation: as no one, who knows what he is about in good company, would venture to talk all; – so no author, who understands the just boundaries of decorum and good breeding, would presume to think all: The truest respect which you can pay your readers' understanding, is to halve this matter amicably, and leave him something to imagine, in his turn, as well as yourself.'[3] Sterne offers here a fine blueprint for hermeneutic dialogue; I would only add, by way of my own readerly rewriting of his text, that the reader will *always* have something to imagine or interpret, whether the author has the good grace to allow for it or not! The imaginative reinterpretation of meaning is not a luxury of literary etiquette but a necessity of textual understanding.

In contrast to the situation of spoken dialogue, limited by the particular *contextualization* of a synchronic discourse between speaking subjects, the textualization of dialogue emancipates meaning from the strict intentions of the authors and creates a new audience which extends diachronically to anyone who can read. As Ricoeur observes in *Hermeneutics and the Human Sciences*: 'An essential characteristic of a literary (i.e. written) work . . . is that it transcends its own psycho-sociological conditions of production and thereby opens itself to an unlimited series of readings, themselves situated in different socio-cultural conditions. In short, the text must be able, from the sociological as well as the psychological point of view, to 'decontextualize' itself in such a way that it can be 'recontextualized' in a new situation – as accomplished, precisely, by the act of reading.'[4] Consequently, in the transition from the spoken to the written word, we find that the Romantic model of dialogue as a pre-established harmony of mutual subjectivities is quite inadequate. The 'textualized' dialogue reveals that language is never purely and simply our own (in the sense of a contemporaneous immediacy, subjective or intersubjective), but always involves the traces and anticipations of *other* language-users, existing in other places and in other times, past and future.

But if the hermeneutic potencies of the *word* undergo such alteration in the transcription of speech into text, what of the *world* about which the authors speak? All discourse, spoken or written, presupposes 'someone saying something to someone about something'.[5] The problem of reference can never be dispensed with altogether. But what happens to reference, we may ask, when spoken discourse becomes a text? In a written dialogue the reference can no longer be limited to the spatio-temporal context of a 'here and now' shared by the interlocutors of a spoken dialogue. All writing, fictional or otherwise, is in some degree a reinscription and reinterpretation of an original context of experience; and to that extent it would seem to eliminate the question of reference. But the matter is not quite so simple. Written discourse certainly abolishes the *first-order reference* to the actual world of experience 'here and now', but this abolition serves in turn to open up a *second-order reference* to the possible worlds proposed by the text. Ricoeur aptly describes this shifting of referential orders as follows:

> The unique referential dimension of the work (as written) . . . raises, in my view, the most fundamental hermeneutical problem. If we can no longer define hermeneutics in terms of the search for the psychological intentions of another person which are concealed *behind* the text, and if we do not want to reduce interpretation to the dismantling of structures, then what remains to be interpreted? I shall say: to interpret is to explicate the type of being-in-the-world unfolded *in front of* the text . . . For what must be interpreted in a text is a proposed world which I could inhabit and wherein I could project one of my own-most possibilities . . . The world of the text is therefore not the world of everyday language.[6]

In respect of the dialogues in this book, we might even speak of a *third-order reference*, in so far as these dialogues involve authors producing dialogical texts *about* their own second-order philosophical texts, which are themselves in some sense *about* a first-order reference to lived experience. (And one might even argue, as Derrida does, that this first-order reference is itself already a text: a pattern of infinitely self-erasing traces or *archi-écriture*.) We may conclude, therefore, that the dialogues contained between these covers are not in fact attempts to retrace the texts of these thinkers back to some 'original' discourse of everyday language or experience. They are texts about texts about texts. This self-confessed parasitism is not, however, intended in the negative sense of alienating or obscuring the meaning of the philosophies at issue. It is not meant in the mimetic sense of being a copy of a copy, invoked by Plato in the *Republic* to denounce literary artefacts as 'poor children of poor parents' (i.e. the text as a mere imitation of natural experience itself construed as a mere imitation of some otherworldly, transcendental truth). Our aim is to deploy the textual reordering of reference as a means of communicating the interpretative horizons of the author's world to the interpretative horizons of the reader's world. Such, at any rate, is our intention. The ultimate proof of the hermeneutic pudding is, of course, in the eating – the response of the reader.

We may ask finally: what becomes of the *subject* (i.e. the author and the reader) in the transition of both *word* and *world* from speech to writing? Each reader of these dialogues will be attempting to reappropriate in some dialectical way the authors' words and worlds expropriated by the very process of textual inscription. Because, however, writing is not some reversible process of first-order referential correspondence, the hermeneutic reappropriation (*Aneignung*) of the reader can never claim to achieve an exact correlation (temporal or intellectual) with the intentional reference of the author. In other words, any reader who enters into genuine dialogue with these texts will in principle experience some change in his own understanding of himself and his world. Once again, I can do no better than recite Ricoeur's own concise account of the reader's dialectic of self-understanding in front of the text:

> (The reader's) appropriation is quite the contrary of contemporaneousness and congeniality: it is understanding at and through distance . . . In contrast to the tradition of the *cogito* and to the pretension of the subject to know itself by immediate intuition, it must be said that we understand ourselves only by the long detour of signs of humanity deposited in cultural works. . . Thus what seems most contrary to subjectivity, and what structural analysis discloses as the texture of the text, is the very medium within which we understand ourselves. . . Ultimately what I appropriate (qua reader) is a proposed world. The latter is not *behind* the text, as a hidden intention would be, but *in front* of it, as that which the work unfolds, discloses, reveals. Henceforth to understand is to *understand oneself in front of the text*. It is not a question of imposing upon the text our finite capacity of understanding, but of exposing ourselves to the text and receiving from it an enlarged self, which would be the proposed existence corresponding in the most suitable way to the world proposed.[7]

One can speak accordingly of the reading process as a 'metamorphosis of the ego' which requires a process of 'distanciation' in the relation of the reader's self to itself. The reader's self-understanding must be seen as a *disappropriation* quite as much as an *appropriation*. And this calls for a dialectical realignment of phenomenological hermeneutics with critical theory: 'A critique of the illusions of the subject, in a Marxist or Freudian manner, therefore can and must be incorporated into self-understanding. . . We can no longer oppose hermeneutics and the critique of ideology. The critique of ideology is the necessary detour which self-understanding must take, if the latter is to be formed by the matter of the text and not by the prejudices of the reader.'[8] This is the decisive juncture at which Ricoeur's hermeneutic analysis overlaps with the ethical critique of Lévinas, the deconstructive analysis of Derrida and the Marxist–Freudian analysis of Marcuse and the Frankfurt school.

While the subject-readers undergo a certain transformation in the reading of these dialogues, so too do the subject-interlocutors who have authored them. For example, my own self-understanding as a dialogical questioner (conditioned by my particular set of cultural, national, religious, philosophical and affective discourses) has had to submit itself to a metamorphosis in the hermeneutic exchange of question-and-answer with the thinkers featured here (each with his own specific discourses). And it is probable that these thinkers themselves have undergone a certain transformation of their respective self-understanding – even if this entails no more than an alternative reformulation of their previously formulated *words* and *worlds*. In short, these texts of dialogue bespeak the transmigration of each author into new horizons of *possible* meaning, horizons which remain open in turn to the *possible* reinterpretations of each reader.

Notes

1. Martin Heidegger, *Erläuterungen zu Hölderlins Dichtung*, 4th edn. Klostermann, Frankfurt, 1971, pp. 38–40.
2. Hans-Georg Gadamer, *Wahrheit und Methode*. Paul Siebeck, Tübingen, 1960, pp. 289 *et seq*.
3. Laurence Sterne, *The Life and Opinions of Tristram Shandy*. Penguin, Harmondsworth, 1967, p. 127.
4. Paul Ricoeur, 'The Hermeneutical Function of Distanciation' in *Hermeneutics and the Human Sciences*, ed. and transl. J.B. Thompson. Cambridge University Press, Cambridge, 1981, p. 139.
5. *Ibid.*, p. 138.
6. *Ibid.*, pp. 141–2.
7. *Ibid.*, p. 144.
8. *Ibid.*, p. 144.